A GRANNY'S GUIDE TO LONDON

BY SHIRLEY EATON

PUBLISHED BY
KENSINGTON WEST PRODUCTIONS LTD
HEXHAM, ENGLAND

Kensington West Productions Ltd
5 Cattle Market, Hexham
Northumberland NE46 1NJ
Tel: (01434) 609933 Fax: (01434) 600066
E Mail: kwp@kensingtonwest.demon.co.uk

Editor - Shirley Eaton

Consultant Editor - Sarah Caisley

Design - Diane Ridley, Nick Ridley

Maps and Illustrations - Phil Anderton, Nick Ridley

Origination - Pre Press Hong Kong

Printing - Liang Yu Printing Factory Hong Kong

Front Cover Picture - Paul Haigh, They're Changing The Guard
Courtesy of - Rosenstiel's

CONTENTS

Natural History Museum

FOREWORD -
THE GRANNY'S GUIDE TO LONDON

Dedicated to five very special people: Tom, James, Alice, Eloise & Olivia.

I have compiled this guide to London for people whose aim is to have fun with children, as much as showing them the sights of London. In case children ask questions, which they invariably do, I am including some B.F.G.s (Boring Facts for Grannies.)

I became a granny living in London at the time that my first grandchild was three. At this time one of my major preoccupations was planning ways to make Tom want to be with me in London as often as possible. As a result I would devise interesting things for him to do that were both fun for him and of interest to me . . . when did you last visit the Science Museum or the excellent London Planetarium? I did not attempt, with him or any of my other grandchildren to be too much of an educationalist, because in my opinion that is not what grandparents are for.

London is one of the most exciting cities in the world for a child. Living in the country as all five of my grandchildren do, the size of everything and the general excitement never fails to get through to them.

This guide offers ideas that will appeal to children from 3 to 15. The age of three is when my children first became aware of the magic of London and, at fifteen sadly I think, Granny's magic (apart from her bank balance) starts to wane.

I have learnt from my ten years experience of being a grandparent in London that there are certain rules you must abide by. The first rule is to give your children a few days warning of an impending visit so they can become excited. Anticipation is an important ingredient in the London experience and it also provides parents with some highly valuable blackmail material.

Secondly, they all seem to enjoy an itinerary which starts from the moment you meet. As we all know, children get tired and time out at home or in a hotel should always be worked into your schedule. Naturally, all children have different points of tiredness but an upset child can ruin the best planned day.

I have had great fun researching this book and it is my genuine hope that at least some of the information is of help to you in looking after children, but more importantly that it gives you a chance to witness them growing up, and between you and me and anybody else that cares to listen, I suggest it keeps a spring in the feet that little bit longer! It also helps enormously to plan your itinerary ahead and, although it's not essential, a dry run before they arrive can make the world of difference.

I'd like to give a big thank you to everyone who has been so encouraging and helpful whilst I have been researching this guide, they have made my job great fun and so rewarding.

The most important thing of all is to enjoy time with children. It is such a special and rewarding relationship. I always say this is the world's best kept secret.

Legoland

HOW TO USE THE BOOK

There are hundreds of guides to London, surely one of the most varied and interesting cities in the world. This book is a personal perspective of a Grandmother who has delighted in enjoying England's capital to the full. It would be wrong to presume that the list is any way complete - it's far more a list of personal observations that will encourage grandparents, parents and all those charged with the responsibility and joy of entertaining the younger generation.

All the information has been checked thoroughly and carefully but it is always sensible to ring in advance for any particular information you may require with reference to admission times and prices as they do vary from season to season. Shirley's comments on the recommended age is a considered one but each reader will decide what's right for their own children - on all occasions we would anticipate children be accompanied.

As you may know, London is often a difficult city in which to drive to say the least. As a result we have tried to advise on the best form of public transport to reach most of our recommended places to

Tower Bridge

visit. Naturally, when it comes to shops and restaurants there are numerous places that we could have mentioned; in most cases we have tried to identify a small number that are particularly good or interesting to children. The museums, galleries, activities and the various other buildings and monuments are, we hope, a particularly diverse selection which should satisfy the most enthusiastic child! We would be delighted to receive any suggestions of ideas for our next edition of the guide. We hope this book helps children and adults of all generations to enjoy the marvellous sights of London - a city which offers history, heritage and activity that all children will delight in.

B.F.G. *Hamleys - If all the soft toys sold by Hamleys in a year were to stand side by side, they would stretch for 66,666 miles.*

More than 8 million Barbie dolls (and family members) have been sold world wide since 1959. Placed head to toe they would circle the earth 6 times.

The earliest Action Man was in fact made 2000 years ago in Ancient Rome when supporters of gladiator teams would buy jointed terracotta mascots of their favourite warriors.

THE GRANNY'S GUIDE ATTRACTIONS OF THE YEAR

(1) The Imperial War Museum
(2) B.B.C. Experience
(3) Science Museum

THE GRANNY'S GUIDE SMALLER ATTRACTIONS OF THE YEAR

(1) Rock Circus
(2) Theatre Museum
(3) Sherlock Holmes Museum

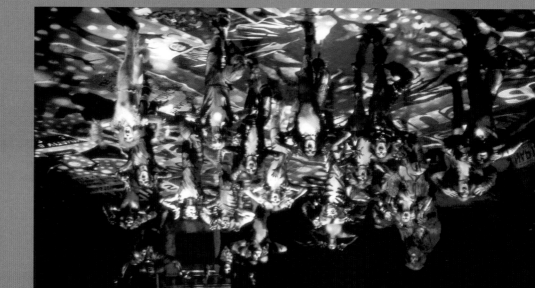

For the three main kinds of entertainment, theatres, films, music, I shall not, on the whole, mention ages because deciding what is suitable for a child has to be up to the individual. To help you choose where to go, what to see, you'll obviously watch the newspapers, most of which have helpful reviews. There are also good what's on weekly magazines. Ask your newsagent for help in choosing what would be best for your needs. If you don't want to buy anything without a look first, go into one of the reference sections of a public library for a browse.

In London the main central ones are:
1. 160 Buckingham Palace Road, Victoria SW1 (tel: 0171 798 2187)
2. Old Town Hall, King's Road, Chelsea SW3 (tel: 0171 352 6056)
3. 35 St. Martin's Street, Westminster WC2 (tel: 0171 798 2036)
4. Marylebone Road, NW1 5PS (tel: 0171 641 1037)

What's on at the theatre is constantly changing, so you need to study what's on offer at the right dates and then judge what the children you are taking would like to see. Naturally children differ greatly in their likes and dislikes. Their ages, their interests and how long they'll be able to sit still are important. In the school holidays, especially Christmas, there are always special productions, such as pantomimes, "Peter Pan", the Roald Dahl stories, "Postman Pat". Some of these get booked up well in advance, so you'll need to plan. Also likely to be popular are the ballet companies' productions of "The Nutcracker" and other well known ballets which could be a big treat for ballet mad little girls and sometimes, these days, boys. Don't make a thing of it, but they might enjoy dressing up in their best clothes. It's sometimes possible to take children into ballet rehearsals. Telephone the theatres where the ballets are showing for information about this. For some types of child this would be a bigger treat than an actual performance , and they needn't dress up!

I have had fun introducing all my grandchildren to theatrical shows of all kinds. The older boys have done all the long established musicals, which will probably be running somewhere for years, such as "Cats", "Phantom of the Opera", "Buddy", etc.

For me, the real thrill of taking grandchildren to the theatre was the big breakthrough from musicals to plays. We started with the long running show "The Mousetrap" which has now run for about 50 years so it must have something. I was taken as a child to see it and we took our children and I'm now taking my grandchildren. As it seems to be an institution, don't overlook it! Another long running play that some children, but by no means all, enjoy is "The Woman in Black".

Find out what's on at the Palladium, which is extremely popular and attracts excellent shows, and check also on the National Theatre where they might be doing productions of "The Wind in the Willows" or other favoured childrens stories. Basically it is safer to go for plays that have been running for some time or that are famous. Do check that the duration is not too long.

Subject to ages, look out for "Grease", "Beowulf", (an Anglo-Saxon tale of dragons and heroes!), "Beauty and the Beast"or other popular children's tales, Disney have started bringing classical stories to the stage and children who have read the books or seen the videos should love these. Also look out for "Show Boat" and "Starlight Express" - the roller skating musical. Visits to Shakespeare plays are often welcomed by older children, particularly if they're doing exams. Think about going to "The Complete Works of William Shakespeare (Abridged)" in which the Reduced Shakespeare Company hurtles through the Bard's 37 plays in amusing style. The same company perform "The Complete History of America (Abridged)" which tells about the 500 years from Columbus to Clinton, a painless history lesson, certainly not right for young children, but okay for older ones who can concentrate. "Les Miserables", the powerful French revolutionary musical, will no doubt be running somewhere and will appeal to many.

Also consider the Open Air Shakespeare productions in Regent's Park. These are always fun and the actors are great with kids who won't get into trouble if they shuffle about. And Marcel Marceau, the French mime king, is brilliant at communicating with most ages, if he happens to be in London. Watch out for what's on at the Young Vic Studio, the Old Vic, the Lyric Theatre, Hammersmith and, if you can get there, The Watermans Arts Centre, Brentford, the beautifully restored Richmond Theatre and the Orange Tree, also in Richmond.

B.F.G's. For full lists of the shows at all the London theatres, which constantly change, the Evening Standard is worth studying for up to date advice. The main London theatres that are usually worth keeping an eye on for children are:

Apollo Victoria, 17 Wilton Road SW1. tel: 0171 416 6070
Barbican Theatre, Silk Street, EC2. tel: 0171 638 8891
Cambridge Theatre, Earlham Street, WC2. tel: 0171 494 5080
Criterion Theatre, Piccadilly Circus, WIV. tel: 0171 369 1747
Dominion Theatre, Tottenham Court Road, W1P. tel: 0171 656 1888
Fortune Theatre, Russell Street, WC2. tel: 0171 836 2238
Her Majesty's Theatre, Haymarket, SW1. tel: 0171 494 5400
London Coliseum, St. Martin's Lane, WC2. tel: 0171 632 8300
London Palladium, Argyll Street, W1. tel: 0171 437 7373
National Theatre, South Bank SE1. tel: 0171 928 2252
New London Theatre, Drury Lane, WC2. tel: 0171 405 0072
Old Vic, Waterloo Road, SE1 tel: 0171928 7616
Orange Tree, Kew Road, Richmond. tel: 0181 940 3633
Palace Theatre, Shaftesbury Avenue, W1V. tel: 0171 434 0909

Phoenix Theatre, Charing Cross Road, WC2. tel: 0171 369 1733
Prince Edward Theatre, Old Compton Street, WIV. tel: 0171 447 5400
Richmond Theatre, The Green, Richmond. tel: 0181 940 0088
Sadler's Wells Theatre, Rosebery Avenue, EC1. tel: 0171 278 8916
St. Martin's Theatre, West Street, WC2. tel: 0171 836 1443
Strand Theatre, Aldwych, WC2. tel: 0171 930 8800
Theatre Royal, Drury Lane, WC2. tel: 0171 836 8108
Victoria Palace, Victoria Street, SW1. tel: 0171 834 1317
Waterman's Arts Centre, Brentford. tel: 0181 568 1176
Young Vic, The Cut, Waterloo, SE1 tel: 0171 928 6363

THE GLOBE THEATRE

Bear Gardens, Bankside, New Globe Wall, London SE1
tel: 0171 902 1500
age group: 12-15
opening times: Monday to Sunday 10am to 5pm
how to get there: by Underground to Mansion House

The Globe is an amazing achievement. The idea was first conceived by the late

Sam Wanamaker to recreate the theatre on the old site as soon as possible to how it was in Shakespeare's time. Zoe Wanamaker lovingly carried on the work after her father died using donations from all parts of the world. There is a museum showing how everything was constructed which is the part older children will enjoy and Shakespeare enthusiasts would enjoy performances as well.

OPEN AIR THEATRE

Regents Park, London NW1 4NP
box office tel: 0171 486 2431/1933
admission: £5 per seat for all ages
how to get there: Underground - Baker Street. Buses - any going to the top of Baker Street and go into the Park at this point – well sign-posted

to the Open Air Theatre.

This is a really Open Air Theatre for adults, but in the summer school holidays, they always put on a production for children, and these take place on Saturday mornings and 2.30pm matinées but it is wise to phone and find out times and suitability of age for these performances.

We went to see The Jungle Book which had a cast of 35, 12 to 16 year olds performing. We luckily picked good weather had a picnic in the park and then saw the play. It was a great outing.

THEATRES SPECIALISING IN PLAYS FOR CHILDREN ARE :

THE POLKA THEATRE

240 The Broadway, Wimbledon, London SW19 1SB
tel: 0181 542 4258
age group: All ages
admission: Varies for each production but £7 per ticket is a good guide
how to get there: Underground - South Wimbledon (Northern Line), Wimbledon (District Line). Buses - 57, 93, 155 stop outside; 131, 156, 163, 200 stop nearby.

A very special theatre which was built exclusively for children and opened by the Queen Mother in 1979. Many large companies have helped to sponsor the theatre and they have recently received a grant from the National Lottery fund. It is easy to get to. We took the tube on the District Line which took about 25 minutes from Central London or you can take the Northern Line to South Wimbledon and you then have a brisk walk for about 10 minutes, or if you wish to be extravagant take a taxi from the station.

The theatre has a great deal going on, workshops in the school holidays and the weekends, children's parties catered for at approximately

£4.95 per child, and then of course the current production in the main theatre which seats 300 and a smaller theatre for 80 which does varied entertainment, phone for information.

I took my 8 year old granddaughter to see 'The House At Pooh Corner' which was a brilliant production. Both Alice and myself sat spellbound for the 2 hour duration of the production. Seats are reasonably priced which is an added bonus.

THE UNICORN THEATRE

Arts Theatre, 6/7 Great Newport Street, London WC2
Box Office No: 0171 836 3334/2132
age group: 4 - 15
admission: £5 to £10 depending on seats
how to get there: Underground - Leicester Square

This is a theatre devoted to children, very easy to get to by tube and just off Leicester Square. Because they are child orientated the productions are never too long and the seats are reasonably priced. You do need information as they do not advertise in the Theatre Guide. They will send you a flyer of what is currently running and coming in the near future. They do workshops for children of all ages in the school holidays and at weekends. The season for productions is from October to April, but phone for help and they are helpful.

I took my three granddaughters to an Irish play. They sat spellbound for well over an hour. It was their first serious excursion to the theatre and I think a good choice.

PUPPET THEATRE

THE LITTLE ANGEL THEATRE

14, Dagmar Passage, Cross Street, London
N1 2DN
tel: Box Office 0171 226 1787
age group: 3 - 11
admission charges: Adults £5.50, OAPs and
Children £4.50
how to get there: Underground - Angel on
the Northern Line, Highbury and Islington
on the Victoria Line. Buses - Essex Road 38,
56, 73, 171A and Upper Street 4, 19, 30, 43

A delightful little theatre, which calls itself "The Home of British Puppetry" with sensational puppet shows, absolute heaven for young children. The performances are mostly on Saturday and Sunday with performances at 11am or 3pm but in the school holidays they do have performances during the week. Phone to find out what is going on. You will find them very helpful. Productions are targeted for specific age groups so when enquiring make sure you ask what age they are catering for. There is nothing worse than taking a 9 year old to something which is aimed at 4 to 6 year olds, and please note, they do not allow children in under the specified age!

(For help in locating London theatres, see maps at the end of the book.)

FILMS

Seeing a film is an ideal choice for a wet day, but conferences will almost certainly be necessary to find out what the children would like to see and they'll probably know more about which films they're allowed to see than you. The Evening Standard is a good source for finding out what's on and at what times. Or you could mosey round W.H. Smith's, where you might decide to buy a video which could end up being cheaper.

ABC Cinema, Swiss Centre Leicester Square W1. tel: 0171 437 2096
Empire Cinema, Leicester Square WC2. tel: 0171 437 1234
Odeon Leicester Square, 22 Leicester Square WC2H tel: 0181 315 4215
Odeon West End, 40 Leicester Square W2H 7LQ. tel: 0181 315 4221
Prince Charles Cinema, Leicester Square WC2. tel: 0171 437 8181
Virgin Haymarket, Haymarket SW1. tel: 0171 839 1527
Warner West End, Leicester Square WC2. tel: 0171 437 4343

ROCK AND POP

Going to a concert could be one of the biggest treats ever if you can manage to find a suitable place to go, although rock and pop shows are mostly at night and therefore only right for older children. Look in the papers to find out what's on but tread carefully before choosing so you don't get into trouble with the children's parents! Also bear in mind that you might find this an ear splitting and expensive experience.

RADIO & TV SHOWS

Young children are not allowed to attend these, but I have found that my older grandchildren enjoy sitting in on recordings of radio and tv shows. By going to these, they are able to see how programmes are made, how many people are involved, how complicated the work can be. Later, of course, they can view or hear the recordings when they go out on air. The shows are usually free, but on the downside you have to book in advance.

The main organisations to contact are:

RADIO - B.B.C.

Radio Ticket Unit, BBC, London WIA 4WW
tel: 0171 765 5243
recorded information; 0171 765 5858 (also on ceefax)
You can either ask to be put on their regular mailing list, or send them an sae for specific enquiries, checking the age of children who will be allowed in.

Most radio shows are recorded at:
1. BBC Radio Theatre, Broadcasting House, London W1
2. Hippodrome, North End Road, London NW11.
3. Maida Vale Studios, Delaware Road, London W9.

Telephone 0171 287 0045 for information on what programmes are being made and find out if they're suitable for your children's ages. Currently children over 15 are being allowed to some recordings and it is hoped in the near future that younger children's recordings will be made on Saturday mornings.

TELEVISION

BBC AUDIENCE SERVICES

Room 301, Design Building, Television Centre, London W12 7RJ
tel: 0181 576 1227

Again be sure to check what ages will be allowed in. You can send an sae to Audience Services for news of programmes being made.

LWT

The London Television Centre, Upper Ground, London SE1 9LT

It took a long time to research all these eateries and most that I have included are aimed at the younger person. New restaurants open almost daily it seems in London and many are Italian pasta places which I have found most children love, and it can be a reasonable meal, so look out for these on your travels.

Nearly all museums have their own catering facilities for visitors and these are mentioned in the Museum section, some are now outstanding but others I have to say, are not good. But do try to work these into your day as it will save time and the aggravation of finding somewhere to eat before visiting your next port of call.

THE BRASSERIE

272 Brompton Road, London SW3
tel: 0171 581 3089
age group: 3 - 15
opening times: Monday to Saturday 8am to ll.30pm

This is one of the original French brasseries in London and has been open for about 20 years. It is great for breakfast, lunch or dinner. The young all adore it and we have voted it the best chips and coffee in London. My favourite comfort food here is egg and chips and for the children the addition of tomato ketchup makes it home from home!

CAFE INTERNET

22/24 Buckingham Palace Road, London SW1
tel: 0171 223 5786
age group:10 - 15
opening times: 7am to 9pm Monday to Friday; 9am to 9pm Saturday; 10am to 9pm Sunday
how to get there: Underground - Victoria Station. Buses - 36, 52

This is the original Internet Cafe. One or two have come and gone but this one remains and seems to be extremely well established and thought of. I took my two grandsons here and although it is not aimed at children, both have a knowledge of computers and consequently enjoyed a hosted half hour training at £10 (quite pricey but they really loved it) for the session, while I relaxed with a sandwich lunch.

THE CAPITAL RADIO CAFÉ

29/30 Leicester Square, London WC2H 7LE
tel: 0171 484 8888
age group: 10 - 14
opening times: Monday to Saturday ll.45am to 12noon, Sundays 12noon to 11pm

You have much choice in Leicester Square but Capital Radio is a little different; everything is bright and coloured and geared to the trendy young. Food is simple, hamburgers, chips etc, but the big attraction is they have a resident disc jockey who operates from a booth in the centre of the restaurant and, providing he has it, he will play any record of your choice. Try this place with the older ones. It is different but very noisy.

CHOY'S

172 King's Road, London SW3
tel: 0171 352 0505
age group: 7 - 14

I mention this Chinese restaurant only as my grandchildren's favourite. There are many others in London to choose from and the Chinese as with many international restaurants welcome children with open arms. The food is expensive but consistently good. We only go in the evening and it is a big treat. We never cram a film or the theatre into such an evening - just a big night out at Choy's.

DAISY & TOM'S RESTAURANT

181 King's Road, London SW3
tel: 0171 352 5000
age group: 1 - 10
opening times: Monday to Friday 10am to 6pm, Saturday 9.30am to 6.30pm, Sunday l2pm to 6pm

This is the restaurant in the toy shop so it is entirely geared to children. There is a soda fountain which looks like a fairground carousel. You sit on bar stools and can have some very imaginative drinks or lunch and there are tables and chairs alongside for more comfortable eating. The menu is for children: small portions and reasonably priced, an eaterie where grown ups are tolerated!

DEAL'S

Chelsea Harbour, London SW6
tel: 0171 352 5887
age groups: 3 - 15
opening times: Monday to Friday 12noon to 3.30pm and 6pm to 1am, Saturday and Sunday 12noon to 11.30pm

I only take my grandchildren here on a Sunday at lunch time because they have a brilliant face painter and a magician. You must book on a Sunday. They do an excellent children's menu, fish fingers or hamburgers served with plenty of chips.

GEALLES FISH RESTAURANT

2 Farmer Street, London W8
tel: 0171 727 7969
age groups: all children love fish and chips!
opening times: Tuesday to Saturday 12noon to 3pm and 6pm to 11pm

One of the most famous fish and chip restaurants in London and if your young friends are into basic food this could be used as a stopping off place. Reduced prices for children's portions.

FASHION CAFE

5/6 Coventry Street, London W1V 7FL
tel: 0171 287 5888
age group: 8 - 14
opening times: Sunday to Thursday 12noon to 12midnight; Friday to Saturday 12noon to 1am
how to get there: Underground - Piccadilly Circus or Leicester Square

This is fashion with a difference. The café was started and is owned by some of the world's top models. While you eat in lovely surroundings you are entertained by a half hour fashion show.

A long catwalk well raised up runs the length of the restaurant and is visible from every table. There are three shows during the day, 12.30, 1.30 and 2.30. In the evening they are at 6.30, 7.30, 8.30 and 9.30.

A great place for the fashion conscious with what's new in fashion dramatically displayed with good lighting and music. The food is middle of the road in both price and quality. It is possible just to purchase a drink and watch.

HÄAGEN DAZS

Leicester Square, London WC2
tel: 0171 287 9577
age groups: 3 - 15
opening times: Monday to Thursday and Sunday 10am to ll.45pm, Friday and Saturday 10am to 12.45pm.

I include this great ice cream parlour because ice cream here is just wonderful. We have our hamburgers at Planet Hollywood or Capital Radio, then wander round the many tourist traps selling photos and stickers etc and round it off with ice cream for all of us and coffee for myself at this establishment.

HARD ROCK CAFÉ

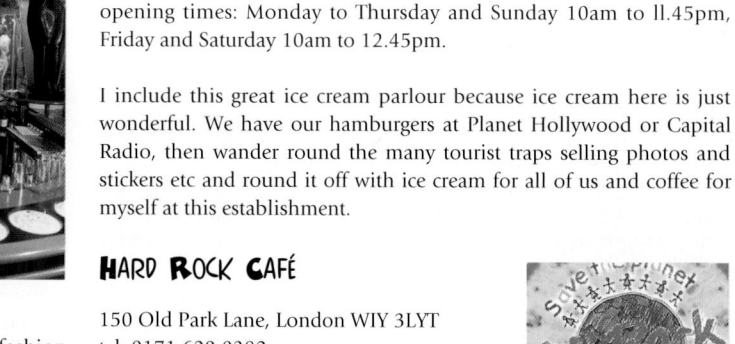

150 Old Park Lane, London WIY 3LYT
tel: 0171 629 0382
age group: 7 - 15
opening times: Monday to Saturday 11.30am to 1am, Sunday 11.30am to 12.30am

This is the original ultimate in hamburger joints. It was the first to open 27 years ago. It has fascinating original music memorabilia, contemporary music and much of interest to keep the young amused. The only drawback is the perpetual long queues so try to choose a quiet time like 11.30am or between 3.30pm and 6.00pm. Children do not like waiting. They also have a merchandise shop which sells T-shirts, jackets, badges, pins, and teddy bears.

HARRODS FOODHALL - BREAKFAST BAR

Knightsbridge, London SW1
tel: 0171 730 1234
age groups: 3 - 15
opening times: Monday, Tuesday, Saturday 10am to 6pm; Wednesday, Thursday, Friday 10am to 7pm; Sunday - only open in December

This is a fun place for breakfast; all ages love this bar, lots of hot chocolate and croissants being BIG favourites.

THE JAM (BUONA SIENA)

289A King's Road, London SW3
tel: 0171 352 8827
age groups: 6 - 15
opening times: Tuesday to Friday 12noon to 3pm and 6pm to 1am, Saturday and Sunday 12noon to 1am, Closed Mondays

This place is quite a novelty as the sitting areas are tiered rather like bunks - hence the name - the top layer of tables being reached by a ladder. The food is not aimed at children but it is quite well priced and one can always find dishes that suit. This I highly recommend for a meal with a difference.

JENNY LO'S NOODLE KITCHEN

14 Eccleston Street, London SW1
tel: 0171 259 0399
age group: 10 - 15

opening times: Monday to Saturday ll.30am to 3pm and 6pm to 10pm, Closed Sundays.

Jenny Lo is the daughter of the late Ken Lo who started Memories of China. Jenny has a great formula. You sit at long tables with everyone from the workman in his boilersuit to the City Slicker. It's cheap, filling and fun.

McDONALD'S

All over London
age group: 3 - 15
opening times: Monday to Sunday 11am to 11pm

I think McDonald's is wonderful, cheap, cheerful, clean, and always a toy or balloon for the child. My grandchildren love the children's meals as they come in a colourful lunch box and include a small toy. My experience here has been that children from the age of 3 - 7 never want to go anywhere else, but after 7 they want something different and I only use it for my older grandchildren as a quick way to fill a corner.

PIZZA EXPRESS

7 Beauchamp Place, London SW3 ING
tel: 0171 589 2355
age group 6 - 15
opening times: Monday to Sunday 12noon to 12midnight

I enjoy Pizza Express myself. There are many pizza places in London but for the adult enjoying a pizza with children Pizza Express is the best and consistently good. Pizza Express has many branches - check with Yellow Pages to find others.

PIZZA IN THE PARK

11 Knightsbridge, London SW1 7LY
tel: 0171 235 5273
age group: 6 - 15
opening times: Monday to Friday 8.30am to 12noon, Saturday and Sunday 9.30am to 12noon

This is a very upmarket pizza restaurant, sophisticated but not too expensive considering it is in Knightsbridge. They are delightful and very welcoming to children.

PLANET HARRODS

Knightsbridge, London SW1
tel: 0171 730 1234
age group: 3 - 15
opening times: Monday, Tuesday, Saturday 10am to 6pm; Wednesday, Thursday, Friday 10am to 7pm; Sunday - only open in December

The food is simple, plenty of chips, good ice creams and cartoons playing non-stop on large screens around this colourful fun restaurant.

PLANET HOLLYWOOD

13 Coventry Street,
London W1V 7FE
tel: 0171 734 6220

age group: 8 - 15
opening times: Monday to Saturday 11.30am to 1pm, Sunday 11.30am to 12.30pm

Great fun, all the excitement of Hollywood and full of interesting film memorabilia which can be viewed such as Silvester Stallone's motorbike, the Terminator and Buzz Lightyear. Large screens are everywhere showing favourite movie clips of the past, present and future. The food's good as well!

RAINFOREST CAFÉ

20 Shaftesbury Avenue, London W1
tel: 0171 434 3111
age group 3 - 15
opening times: Sunday to Thursday 12noon to 11pm, Friday 12noon to 12midnight, Saturday 11.30am to 12midnight

This is quite definitely a most unusual restaurant situated at the

Piccadilly Circus end of Shaftesbury Avenue and within easy reach of many of the places to visit mentioned in this book. All age groups will be happy here. The front of the establishment sells T-shirts and other memorabilia You enter the restaurant by way of a grotto almost expecting to find Father

Christmas at the other end, but instead you enter into an artificial rainforest with tables. Behind trees and undergrowth there are animals that you would expect to find in a rainforest, such as large chimps, monkeys, birds, snakes and giant sized butterflies. Every 15 minutes when thunder and lightning are artificially produced, these mechanical animals come to life for a minute or two. You must have children with you: not a place to have a quiet meal! Fun and central, large queues at the weekend and at holiday times - pick an early or late lunch.

THE RITZ HOTEL

150 Piccadilly, London WIV 9DG
tel: 0171 493 8181
age group: 6 - 15

This is the great afternoon tea experience. The girls love to dress up to fit the lavish surroundings. Boys can be filled up at cheaper establishments! It is seriously expensive so make sure they are very hungry and make it an occasion!

They have two sittings for tea at 3.30 and 5 o'clock and you must book a month in advance as it is so popular.

SMOLENSKY'S DOVER STREET

1 Dover Street, London WI
tel: 0171 491 1199
age group: 3 - 10
opening times: Monday to Saturday 12noon to 12midnight, Sunday 12noon to 10.30pm

Great on Saturdays and Sundays when they have an American family brunch between 1pm and 3pm which is popular with children and there is entertainment in the form of a table-side magician, but be warned it is expensive although very recommendable. With the entertainment it is always advisable to book .

What's more try **Smolensky's on the Strand** - it's fantastic for children with great toys, games, face painting and special meals - a great treat.

Sports Café

80 Haymarket, London SW1Y 4TQ
tel: 0171 839 8300
age group: 10 - 15
opening times: Monday to Wednesday 12noon to 1am Thursday to

Saturday. 12noon to 3am. Sunday 12noon to 10.30pm

This is paradise for football crazy children, the whole restaurant is geared up to sport but mainly football, rugby and American ball games. My 12 year old described it as the 'coolest restaurant in London'.

Everywhere you look there are very large television screens and some smaller ones. Most of the tables have small game consoles. The café is on two levels and on the first floor there is a pool table which can be played on free. On the ground floor there is a basketball net - yet again free.

From an adult point of view this could be a most unsociable venue but it is a very popular choice for all sports mad fans.

There is a reasonably priced children's menu so all in all it is worth a try.

Sticky Fingers

1a Phillimore Gardens, Kensington London W8 7EG
tel: 0171 938 5338
age group: 5 - 15

opening times: Monday to Saturday 12noon to 11.30pm, Sunday closes at 11pm

This restaurant was started and is still owned by Bill Wyman. The name is clever and it is very much the family restaurant and they always run a children's menu. On Sundays there is a magician who appears at 1pm.

THAI POT EXPRESS

148 The Strand, London WC2 1AB
tel: 0171 497 0904
age group 10 - 15
opening times: Monday to Saturday 12noon to 3pm and 5.30pm to 11.15pm Closed Sundays.

Good Thai food, but not too sophisticated. I have been only once with my grandsons and it was voted a winner - and they are very fussy!

PLACES TO STAY

London abounds with hotels and guest houses in most price ranges and I am going to list a few unusual ones which might be useful. Otherwise it is better to contact the London Tourist Board on 0171 932 2000, who will send you an information pack on London which will help you or alternatively you can call into one of the centres. The main one is at Victoria Station forecourt. There are often good value breaks at weekends when hotels are less busy and Ceefax or Teletext often have some really great bargains. The bigger chains may not offer the character of some London hotels but they often provide good facilities and rates for children. Remember always ask for the best bedrooms because if you don't ask you don't get!

PIPPA POP-INS

430 Fulham Road, London SW6 1DU
tel: 0171 385 5706
how to get there: Underground - Fulham Broadway. Buses - 11, 14, 211

Pippa Pop-ins was started by Pippa Deakin in 1992 as a children's hotel and a place where children from 2 - 12 can be looked after 24 hours a day, 7 days a week.

There is a nursery school for 2 to 5 year olds. They can stay for just mornings or all day. Then there is the overnight nursery which is a wonderful idea because here a child can be left for one night or a week and they can accommodate up to 12 children. On the day I visited a little family of two had arrived from Singapore and were being looked after for a week while their parents went house hunting in the country. Another service offered is 'after school'. This is when a child will be picked up from his or her school, given tea and homework supervised if necessary and then wait to be picked up by a parent.

Pippa, and her mother Joyce Deakin who looks after much of the administration and daily running of the establishment are both very innovative. They run outside activities in the holidays and weekends for all ages up to 12 and workshops at the house. When I read the list of some of the planned excursions I was amazed at the wide scope covered.

The house is beautifully decorated both inside and out. The front of the tall Georgian house is yellow and the inside a riot of tasteful colours, any child staying here could only leave happy.

Joyce showed me around and I was impressed at the warm happy atmosphere which pervades everywhere. The day I went it was bursting at the seams with children, some being read stories, some having lunch and some resting.

Pippa has won several awards with this unique concept and in 1995 won the Which Hotel of the Year award. I did feel that Pippa Pop-ins needed to have a special mention in the Granny's Guide to London because if one has grandchildren for a few days one might have a situation when you needed a little help and where better than in the capable hands of Pippa and her well qualified staff.

Do write or phone for a brochure. You will find everyone so willing to help.

THE BULLDOG CLUB

14 Dewhurst Road, London W14
tel: 0171 371 3202
Contact Name: Maggie Jackson

This is a small organisation run by Maggie Jackson who has several houses and flats in London which take in paying guests and treat them as one of the family. You have to pay a small membership fee but once a member always a member. Some of the houses do not cater for children but those that do will make them feel very welcome. Prices vary starting at £75 for a single room up to £95 for a double.

UPTOWN RESERVATIONS

50 Christchurch Street, Chelsea, London SW3 4AR
tel: 0171 351 3445

This is a larger but similar organisation to the Bulldog Club but there is no membership fee. They have about 70 upmarket privately hosted homes in the centre of London with prices for a single at £63 per night to £83 for a double. They also have one bedroom apartments and studios which cost from £275 to £360 per week.

They are registered with the London Tourist Board and have a website for more information.

WOLSEY LODGES

9 Market Place, Hadleigh, Nr Ipswich, Suffolk IP7 5DL
tel: Brochure line 01473 827500
administration 01473 822058

A unique organisation with private homes all over Great Britain. The brochure can only be obtained by writing or phoning. It is free and has information on all 250 of the houses of which about 10 are in London. Here you are treated as one of the family and you can book direct with your host. Most of the London houses will do an evening meal. This is a good idea if you have small children and have to stay in for the evening.

DOLPHIN SQUARE HOTEL AND FLATS

Chichester Street, London SW1
tel: 0171 834 3800

Dolphin Square is in a very central position. You can stay in the hotel or take a small flat, it will not be cheap but fun for the children and they are able to use the hotel's indoor swimming pool. If you take one of the Flats or Studios you have the added advantage of a place to relax and a small kitchen to cook the children a meal.

At the other end of the market, and bearing in mind I am only mentioning accommodation in Central London, there are small hotels in Bayswater, the Cromwell Road and Sussex Gardens where it is possible to get a basic family room for around £70 per night for all of you.

THOMAS COOK

Main Concourse, British Rail Euston Station, London SW5
tel: 0171 388 7435

Thomas Cook offer a booking service for hotels covering a wide range of prices, offices in most of the main line railway stations.

I mention most of the well known London toy shops. I have tried to find a few small unusual ones as these are the ones that I enjoy exploring for the toy that is unconventional and different.

So much selling today is in the packaging and once that is destroyed there seems to be nothing left. Children sadly always fall for this type of marketing so it is up to you to guide them to the toys that are not mindless but instructive, as well as being fun.

Some of the book shops I mention later in this chapter are excellent and the smaller the shop the better personal service can sometimes be found.

I have not included clothes shops in the guide because there is such a large selection in London it would be hard to know where to start - would it be Harrods or Mothercare?

DAISY & TOM

181 King's Road, London SW3
tel: 0171 352 5000
age group: 3 - 10
opening times: Monday to Friday 10am to 6pm, Wednesday to 7pm, Saturday 9.30am to 6.30pm, Sunday 12noon to 6pm

This store is on two floors and is a complete childrens department store. Everything about it is beautifully done and thought out. My three granddaughters find it the ultimate. Every conceivable type of interesting colourful and imaginative toys are on sale, all brilliantly displayed, there are over 6500 titles in the galleried book room, videos, and clothes and shoes that any Granny would find it hard to resist.

The hairdressing salon has a large choice of videos which the child is allowed to choose when having his or her hair cut. A first haircut certificate is offered. In the clothes department, there is an automated puppet show which even I found myself compelled to watch! The restaurant and soda fountain are described in the Eateries section.

I give this shop 10 out of 10 - this is the first one in London but others are planned to open.

EARLY LEARNING CENTRE

(a) Kensington High Street, London W8
(b) King's Road, London SW3
age group: 3 - 10
opening times: Monday to Saturday 9am to 6pm

There are quite a few branches in London and an enormous one in Kensington High Street and a good one on King's Road. There are a few things for them to play with here and also somewhere for Granny to sit! To have an hour here is quite an experience.

GOSH

39 Great Russell Street, Covent Garden, London WC1

tel: 0171 636 1011
age group: 10 - 14
opening times: Saturday to Wednesday 10am to 6pm, Thursday and Friday 10am to 7pm
how to get there: Underground - Russell Square, Holborn and Tottenham Court Road. Buses - 7, 73, 29, 38, 19

A most unusual shop which I stumbled on quite by chance. It is packed with comics for all ages. You might just have a grandchild hooked on comics and wouldn't you be popular knowing about this shop!

HAMLEY'S

Regent Street, London W1
age group: 3 - 10
opening times: Monday, Tuesday, Wednesday, Friday 10am to 7pm, Thursday 10am to 8pm, Saturday 9am to

7pm, Sunday 12noon to 6pm

The most famous toy shop in the world. There are seven floors with every conceivable toy - exhausting but fun.

HARRODS

Knightsbridge, London SW1
tel: 0171 730 1234
age group: 3 - 10
opening times: Monday, Tuesday, Saturday 10am to 6pm; Wednesday, Thursday, Friday 10am to 7pm; Sunday - only open in December

Perhaps the most magical store for children and for mine it is always where they want to go. We start with the moving staircase. . . . . . it has been known to take anything up to an hour of escalating to achieve complete boredom and of course it is free! Level four is the toy department and this is also good for anything up to an hour it's difficult to refuse buying anything - the choice is excellent

On the fourth floor next door to the toys is a restaurant, Planet Harrods - described in the Eateries section.

Having done all this, you still have many other options for entertaining children in Harrods, maybe a haircut if the parents agree and if it is a first haircut at Harrods you get a certificate. Children always love this. Don't forget the lifts, they're big and expansive and if experiencing lifts for the first time where better than Harrods.

Our final port of call is the food department. Here the fish counter has well presented displays appealing to children. The bakery and cake section have birthday cakes which they love viewing and you can round it all off with milk shakes or ice creams sitting on high bar stools at the counter, before finally leaving exhausted!

A couple of months before Christmas, Harrods has a very important date with Father Christmas. He comes in a cavalcade on the first Saturday in November. The roads round Harrods are closed off and it is quite a spectacle. Phone Harrods to check times of Father Christmas's arrival. He can be visited in the run up to Christmas Eve.

PATRICK'S

Lillie Road, London SW6 7SX
tel: 0171 385 9864
age group: 3 - 12
opening times: Monday to Saturday 9.15am to 5.45pm

Small and compact, but an interesting toy shop.

THE SINGING TREE

69 New Kings Road, London SW6 4SQ
tel: 0171 736 4527
age groups: (mostly girls) 3 - 15
opening times: 10am to 5.30pm Monday to Saturday

One of the first specialist dolls house and dolls house accessory shops in London, it has been open for over 20 years. They pride themselves on everything being British made and mostly hand made.They also have a mail order catalogue which will cost you £5.00 including postage. This is a truly outstanding little shop, which is heaven for most little girls.

THE SPY CATCHER

25G Lowndes Square, London SW1
tel: 0171 245 9445
age group: 10 - 15
opening times: Monday to Friday 10am to 6pm, Saturday 10am to 5pm

This shop is a serious spy shop catering in bullet-proof vests, tracking equipment and bodyguard equipment. You can purchase two way sunglasses so you can see who is following you, invisible ink, listening devices, etc etc, so you can imagine just how much children love it, especially the boys. I have taken mine on numerous occasions and the staff are so helpful - no need for them to be in adult shops.

TOWER RECORDS

1 Piccadilly Circus, London W1
tel: 0171 439 2500
age group 7 - 15
opening times: Monday to Saturday 9am to 12midnight, Sunday 12noon to 6pm

Great place to find CD's, tapes and videos etc. Well laid out and can be incorporated into a visit to Segaworld.

TROTTER'S

34 King's Road, London SW3
tel: 0171 259 9620

age group 3 - 10
opening times: Monday to Saturday 9am to 6.30pm, Sunday 10am to 6pm; Late night Wednesday till 7pm

This is almost next door to the Early Learning Centre in the Kings Road and their other branch is in Kensington High Street.

Trotter's is basically a childrens clothes shop, the owners got it right as it is very much geared to the child. There is an honesty juice bar in the middle of the small library of childrens books and we always end up here reading a story and having our juice!

The shoe section, because one can hardly call it a department, has a huge wooden train and the children adore clambering all over this.

VIDEO DEPARTMENT AT HARRODS

Knightsbridge, London SW1
tel: 0171 730 1234

age group: 7 - 15
opening times: Monday, Tuesday, Saturday 10am to 6pm; Wednesday, Thursday, Friday 10am to 7pm; Sunday - only open in December

This is one of the best laid out video departments I have ever seen and believe me I have been to many! The staff are helpful and it is a good place to browse.

HAPPY RETURNS

36 Rosslyn Hill, London NW3
tel: 0171 435 2431
age group: all ages
opening times: Monday to Friday 9.30am to 5.30pm, Saturday 10am to 6pm, Sundays 12.pm to 5.30pm

Excellent shop if you are planning a party. Everything seems bright and cheerful - balloons with names and ages, party bags, in fact everything for a childrens' party and they also have a few toys.

THE LONDON DOLLS HOUSE COMPANY

29 The Market, Covent Gardenm, London   WC2 8RE
tel: 0171 240 8681
age group: 3 - 15
opening times: Monday to Saturday 10am to 7.pm, Sundays 12noon to 5pm

This is the place to buy your Doll's House - such a good selection at all prices. All the accessories you might need to furnish your dolls house can be found here and also many books on the subject. They operate a mail order service and catalogue at £3.80 inclusive of postage and packaging.

DRAGONS

23 Walton Street, London SW3
tel: 0171 287 6558
opening times: Monday to Saturday 10am to 8pm, Sunday 12noon to 6pm

Lots of hand painted, custom made furniture for the perfect nursery, all beautifully displayed. This really is the place to go if you want a very special piece of furniture or even pieces of furniture. If you are lacking in confidence over your interior design abilities, a full 'nursery interior design' service is available.Dragons also supply good individual baby presents for that special occasion when you want something different.

TOYS 'R' US

Trojan Way, Croydon, London
tel: 0181 686 3133
age group: all ages
opening times: Monday to Thursday 9am to 8pm, Friday & Saturday 9pm to 9pm.
A supermarket toy shop. There are branches all over the UK but this is the nearest to Central London. Not really a shop for an unusual wooden toy but has a huge selection of most kinds of children's toys, books,videos and also baby equipment at competitive prices.

HILL TOY COMPANY

71 Abingdon Road, London W8 6AW
tel :0171 937 8797
age group: 3 - 10
opening times: Monday to Friday 9.30am to 5.30pm, Saturday 10am to 5pm

An imaginative, small and friendly shop where children are free to play with many of the toys on display. They have an excellent selection of very appealing dressing up clothes which make fantastic presents and also have a comprehensive mail order side.The Hill Toy Company really caters for children up to the age of 10.

TRIDIAS

25 Bute Street, South Kensington, London SW7
tel: 0171 584 2330
age group: 3 - 12
opening times: Monday to Friday 9.30am to 6pm, Saturday 10am to 6pm

A small shop off Bompton Road and near South Kensington underground station, selling mostly wooden toys and puzzles. There is a range of jewellery bead kits and hair bands that little girls will love. They also produce a mail order catalogue.

CHILDRENS BOOK SHOPS

DAISY & **T**OMS - an excellent well laid out department store devoted to children.

HARRODS - childrens book department is just adjacent to the toys on the 4th floor with a huge selection of books to choose from.

NOMADS **B**OOKS

781 Fulham Road, London SW6 5HA
tel: 0171 736 4000
opening times: Monday - Friday 9am to 8pm, Saturday 10am to 6pm, Sunday 11am to 5pm

This is essentially a book shop for adults but it does have an interesting and comprehensive children's area.

CHILDREN'S **B**OOK **C**ENTRE

237 Kensington High Street, London W8
tel: 0171 937 7497
age groups: 3 months to 15 years.
how to get there: Underground - Kensington High Street. Buses - 9, 10, 27, 28, 29
opening times: Monday to Saturday 9.30am to 6.30pm, Sunday 12noon to 6.30pm

I love this shop as it has a lot to offer, they do have some toys videos etc but it is mostly books. On Saturday morning there are free computer lessons for children. The Book Centre is advertised as catering for children from 3 months to 14 years.

BOOKS FOR CHILDREN

97 Wandsworth Bridge Road, London SW6 2TD
tel: 0171 384 1821
opening times: Monday 10am to 6pm, Tuesday to Friday 9.30am to
6pm, Saturday 9.30am to 5.30pm.

This is the only shop I will mention in any detail as is it is exceptional.
Diane Wolfe-Murray the owner adores children. She herself is a granny
many times over and feels many of them do her customer research for
her. She is a real enthusiast and nothing is too much trouble for her.
Her staff are also extremely helpful and knowledgeable and willing to
help you choose suitable books for all ages and interests.

The other large book shops such as Waterstones, W.H.Smiths,
Blackwells, Dillons, Books etc and the world famous one off Foyles in
Charing Cross Road all now seem to have good childrens sections.

A number of independent shops specialise in Children's titles

including:

Word Play - 1 Broadway Parade, Crouch End,
London N8 9TB tel: 0181 347 6700

Children's Bookshop - 29 Fortis Green Road, Muswell Hill,
London N10 3HP tel: 0181 444 5500

Stoke Newington Bookshop - 159 Stoke Newington High Street,
London N16 0NY tel: 0171 249 2808

Bookends (also paper crafts) - 1/3 Exhibition Road, S. Kensington,
London SW7 7HE tel: 0171 589 2285

Women & Children First - 14 The Market, Greenwich,
London SE10 9HZ tel: 0181 853 1296

The Bookworm - 1177 Finchley Road,
London NW11 0AA tel: 0181 201 9811

In many countries you pay the earth to go round museums and galleries but many in London are free so I recommend making the most of them. What's more it appears that many more will become free if a recent Government initiative is put in place.

There is a wonderful selection on offer and practically all are trying to capture the interest of the younger generation. On researching this section I have been overwhelmed by the enthusiasm of those who work in museums and the different ways they get the young to participate often with activity sheets or a hands-on approach. Workshops that are often organised at weekends and during school holidays are great fun and worth considering.

Long gone are the days when museums consisted of glass cases with the young very bored by the exhibits. These days everything is explained with computers, videos and displays and a great sense of colour and design.

When planning your outings, do make phone calls to find out whether they have workshops or if there is a special event planned for the children. Nine times out of ten you will find everyone is helpful.

I have made a point of mentioning the catering facilities obtainable in nearly all of the museums and galleries because in the last year or so they have improved, in many cases out of all recognition, and if you can incorporate food into a visit it saves hassle and gives you a rest.

BANK OF ENGLAND MUSEUM

Threadneedle Street, London EC2R 8AH
tel: 0171 601 5545
age group: 10 - 15
admission: free
opening times: Monday to Friday 10am to 5pm, Closed public & bank holidays
how to get there: Underground - Bank. Buses - 9, 11, 22.
Do try this one - best of all it's a freebie and

it's easy to get to the City by taking the underground to the Bank or alternatively you get fine views from the top of a bus! There is a certain impressive glamour about the Bank of England which children will never forget. And you can point out papers relating to George Washington and even to Kenneth Grahame who wrote "The Wind in the Willows" and used to work in the Bank.

To my grandchildren, the area they enjoyed most was the Dealing Desk with its up-to-the-minute information displayed on the screens. There's also a telephone commentary which gives an explanation of the work of a dealer on the Foreign Exchange (I have to add that I learnt an awful lot!)

B.F.G. *The Bank is the second largest gold repository in the world after Fort Knox in the United States and children certainly get a thrill from knowing they're walking above a sea of gold bullion.*

BETHNAL GREEN MUSEUM OF CHILDHOOD

Cambridge Heath Road, London E2

tel: 0181 980 2415 - this number connects you to an excellent information line
age group: 5 - 10
admission: free
how to get there: Underground - Bethnal Green (Central Line, one stop east from Liverpool Street).
Buses - 106, 253, 309, D6 to Cambridge Heath Road; 8 to Roman Road; 26, 48, 55 to Hackney Road

The museum is part of the Victoria and Albert Museum and is totally dedicated to toys. They have one of the finest collections of old and new doll's houses I have ever seen and a unique collection of old dolls and Teddy Bears.

At the weekend and in the school holidays there are workshops for children and very informally run. The Saturday I was there we finished up making paper flowers and joining in the Mad Hatter's Tea party with the White Rabbit hosting it. There is a small café with a simple menu and fun cardboard boxes for the children.

Easy to get to, it is literally across the road from the underground so none of this "How far have we got to walk?"

THE BRITISH LIBRARY

96 Euston Road,
London NW1 2DB
tel: 0171 412 7332
age group: 7 - 15
admission: Free
opening times: Monday,
Wednesday, Thursday &
Friday 9.30am to 6pm,
Tuesday 9.30am to 8pm,
Friday & Saturday 9.30am
to 5pm, Sunday 11am to
5pm

how to get there: Underground - Euston & Kings Cross. Buses - 73,10, 32, 91 pass the building

The new British Library can be described as a unique and interesting building. Designed by Sir Colin St John Wilson it has cost a mere £511 million and was officially opened in June 1998. Everyone should see this amazing bit of English architecture and make up their own minds as to whether they like it or not. As we go to press they are currently getting over 1,000 visitors each day.

Here you can see Shakespeare's First Folio and the Magna Carta displayed in such a clever way that it captures children's imagination. There are three galleries, all brilliantly displayed and lit. In the Pearson Gallery there is a section on the story of writing and children's books with a small video explaining and telling stories to the young. They also hold children's activities during the school holidays but this is their first season so please telephone for any information you may need.

For older children there is the opportunity to design a page for a book using the latest technology in publishing - it is an incredible process and absolutely fascinating.

The catering facilities are excellent with a cafeteria style restaurant offering reasonably priced dishes in an atmosphere reminiscent of a reading room, combining a wall of books in a modern setting with lighting which bridges the gap between the two. This part of the library closes at 3.30pm (5pm at weekends) but there is another café below selling sandwiches, soft drinks, coffee etc, all much cheaper than typical motorway cafés.

The gift shop here is aptly named 'The Book Shop' and has a wonderful collection of books.

THE BRITISH MUSEUM

Great Russell Street, London WC1B 3DG
tel: 0171 636 1555
age group: 10 - 15
admission: Free
opening times: Monday to Saturday 10am to 5pm, Sunday 12noon to 6pm. Closed for New Year's Day, Christmas Day Christmas Eve and Boxing Day

how to get there: Underground - Tottenham Court Road, Holborn, Russell Square. Buses - No. 7 stops outside. Others - 8, 73, 24, 188, 38 They are not that well catered for but occasionally in the summer holiday there are workshops attached to an exhibition for children, but I would advise that you telephone before you go.

This is more of a museum for adults but it is a great British Institution and some children might like to visit it. The Japanese galleries are cool and scenic, the library books have now been moved to the British Library and the bronzes and sculptures are excellent. Childrens activity sheets and trails are available, ask at the information desk.

There is a good café/restaurant serving imaginative food at reasonable prices and I enjoyed going to the childrens shop where they have activity packs and pocket sized souvenirs.

CABARET MECHANICAL THEATRE

33/34 Covent Garden, London WC2 8RE
tel: 0171 379 7961

age group: 4 - 15

admission: Adults £1.95 Children & OAPs £1.20. Children under 5 are free

opening times: Monday to Saturday 10am to 6.30pm Sunday 11am to 6.30pm

how to get there: Underground - Covent Garden, Strand Buses

The first thing to remember here is it is difficult to find but once found you can have an intriguing and amusing time.

The museum itself is located within the market at Covent Garden and is at basement level at the end of a row of fascinating little shops. There are two parts to the whole. One part is the museum itself which consists of 64 handmade automata - all built this century - which come to life at the touch of a button. All displays are cleverly lit and steps can be carried to aid viewing for smaller children.

The second part is a shop selling automata in kit form for children and adults to build. There are also a few ready assembled pieces and prices range from £1.50 to £180. You can also see some larger, one off machines which are coin operated and fascinating. The antiques of the future?

The Cabaret Mechanical Theatre operates a mail order service and it is worth asking them to send you a catalogue before you go.

On the day I went I took my 8 year old granddaughter who loved the museum so much she had to be dragged away. We then enjoyed a drink in the small plaza where you can have coffee, orange juice and wines.

CABINET WAR ROOMS

Clive Steps, King Charles Street,
London SW1
tel: 0171 930 6961
age group: 12 - 15
admission: Adults £4.60, OAPs £3.40,
Children £2.30

opening times: Daily except 24-26 December 10am to 6pm
how to get there: Underground - St James's Park or Westminster.
Buses - 3, 11, 12, 24, 53, 77A, 88, 109, 159, 184, 211.

When visiting the War Rooms be sure that your youngsters have some knowledge of the second World War and Winston Churchill. It is a museum that older boys and girls will be most interested in, as you will be too. The rooms are the original headquarters, largely left as they were during the war and in some cases practically untouched since 1945. The fascination to me is the basic communications and the direct line to the White House and Washington. My goodness what progress since, if that is what we can call it!

THE BRITAIN AT WAR EXPERIENCE

64-66 Tooley Street, London SE1
0171 403 3171
age group: 10 - 15
admission: Adults £5.95, OAPs £3.95, Children £1.50

opening times: April - September Monday to Sunday 10am to 5.30pm; October - March Monday to Sunday 10am to 4.30pm
how to get there: Underground - to London Bridge, the Water Bus and tour buses pass the door

This is a small museum which lives up to its title. You are sent down to a wartime underground in a lift and immediately are into the conditions that so many experienced during the air raids in London. It's extremely well done and my children had a much better idea of what the war was like after this 40 minute visit. You witness an enemy attack overhead and have to take cover in an Anderson Shelter. You listen to messages from wartime leaders in the BBC radio studio and even dance with American GIs in the Rainbow Room. There are sometimes wartime dressing up sessions when children can put on gas masks, tin helmets and uniforms, or wartime treasure trails. You finish up walking through a bombed house with all the rubble and the noise of sirens. This visit can be combined with the many other things to do in this area - but never forget don't try to do too much.

CHARLES DICKENS' HOUSE

48 Doughty Street, London WC1
tel: 0171 405 2127
opening times: Monday to Friday 9.45am to 5.30pm, Saturday 10am to 5pm
age group: 12 - 15
admission: Adults £3.50, OAPs £2.50, Children £1.50
how to get there: Underground - Russell Square. Buses - 17, 18, 19, 45, 46, 171, 171A, 196, 243, 503, 505.

If children have read any of Charles Dickens novels, or seen any of the films based on them, they might enjoy experiencing a visit to the author's former home. When he moved here, "Pickwick Papers" was being issued in monthly parts and was so famous that people could go out and buy a Mr Pickwick hat, or a Mr Pickwick walking stick, or a box of Pickwick cigars. Originally Dickens was published under the pen-name of "Boz",but while at Doughty Street he began to use his own name when he wrote "Oliver Twist" and "Nicholas Nickleby".

This is the house that Dickens lived in for nearly three years from 1837 to 1839. It has been lovingly kept up and for the more interested child it has some fascinating things to see, like several of the author's belongings and the family tree and many artefacts.

FLORENCE NIGHTINGALE MUSEUM

2 Lambeth Palace Road, London SE1 7EW
tel: 0171 620 0374
age groups: 10 - 15
admission: Adults £3.50, OAPs and Children (5-18) £2.50
opening times: 10am to 5pm Tuesday to Saturday (last admission 4pm)

how to get there: Underground - to Westminster & Waterloo. Buses - 12, 53, 77, 109, 171, 171A, 507, 511, C1

The Florence Nightingale Museum is at St Thomas's Hospital just over Westminster Bridge. Don't attempt to bring the car. I think buses are the best option as most pass the door and it is about 10 mins walk from Westminster tube station.

If you have a child who wants to take up nursing or is in any way fascinated by the subject then this is the museum to visit.

I visited the museum on my own without having any young to fill the requirements of a visit and what I enjoyed most was the 20 minute video on the life of Florence Nightingale that remarkable lady and a pioneer in nursing - it was brilliantly done. She completely reformed nursing and established the profession in 1860 and it was here at St Thomas's Hospital where it all started - what an achievement.

The museum offers only a few items for children in the summer holidays as they are short staffed but at Christmas they create a Victorian Christmas as the Nightingale family and others would have spent it. During half terms they do children's first aid courses and design a modern nurses uniform, just a few activities I was told about. There is also a Florence Nightingale questionnaire which the children answer as they go around the museum.

No catering facilities or shops are on the premises, but guide books, pencils and note books can be bought on the way out.

GEFFRYE MUSEUM

Kingsland Road, London E2 8EA
tel: 0171 739 9893
age groups: 8-15
admission: Free
opening times: Tuesday to Saturday 10am to 5pm, Sundays and Bank Holidays 2pm to 5pm. Open all year except Mondays, Christmas Eve, Christmas Day, Boxing Day, New Year's Day and Good Friday.

how to get there: Underground - Liverpool Street then buses - 149 or 242 or Old Street, exit 2, then bus 243.

The Museum is housed in a row of 18th century almshouses which lend themselves well to this series of period rooms which are replicas of those spanning the centuries, 1600 to the modern day. Each room is exceptionally well done and gives a fascinating insight into how our lives and lifestyles have changed so dramatically over time.

The Museum is soon to be expanded to double its current size. There is a small but pretty garden where you can picnic and a small café serving hot drinks and soft drinks. The Museum runs workshops for children during the school holidays but it is advisable to telephone in advance for details. The Museum is not the most accessible by public transport but there are plenty of car parking spaces around the Museum.

HORNIMAN MUSEUM

London Road,London SE23

tel: 0181 699 1872
age group: 8 - 15
opening times: Monday to Saturday 10.30am to 5.30pm, Sunday 2pm to 5.30pm
how to get there: by train to Forest Hill.

This is a strange mixture as it includes both natural history items and musical instruments. If your children are musicians and they enjoy the natural history programmes on TV they might be interested in this museum. There are occasional workshops and music, so ring to find out what is going on.

THE IMPERIAL WAR MUSEUM

Lambeth Road, London SE1 6HZ
age group: 8 - 14
tel: 0171 416 5320 for enquiries, 0891 600 140 (recorded)
opening times: All year Monday to Saturday 10.am to 6pm, Closed

December. 24th, 25th, 26th
admission: Adults £4.70, Children Under 16 £2.35, OAPs & Students £3.70. The Museum is free to all after 4.30pm.
how to get there: Underground - Waterloo or Elephant & Castle and it is approximately a 20 minute walk from both stations. Buses - 1, 3, 12, 45, 53, 63, 159, 169, 171

The Imperial War Museum may sound like a boring museum from its title but is far from it. We had a good time. I took two grandsons, the older of whom had been studying the two world wars at school as part of his syllabus. If you need to know anything pre the First World War you must concentrate on the National Army Museum (see page 57).

They are very keen to please the young and when we went there, there was a Spy School Training Mission where they had to fill in a quiz to keep their interest and to help them absorb much more information about the various exhibits.

To me, one of the most fascinating parts was the Trench Experience. I have seen this in other museums but not as well done as here. In fact, the boys thought it was horrifying that soldiers went through such things in the First World War. There are many videos, telephone tapes and a small cinema. But one of the things we especially enjoyed was The Secret War: a permanent exhibition about espionage and special agents - find me a young child that does not love all this.

The café here is excellent, one of the best I have come across. Self service in a tasteful, modern environment. Lunch is above average and joy of joys, cream teas!
You can bring a picnic as the grounds are well served with tables and chairs. If you choose to take the car there are plenty of meters around the area.

We only allowed ourselves a couple of hours here but with food thrown in you could easily extend your visit. The shop is excellent, original gifts targeted at the two world wars.

KEW BRIDGE STEAM MUSEUM

Green Dragon Lane, Brentford,
Middlesex TW8 0EN
tel: 0181 568 4757

age group: 7 -15

opening times: All the year round
Monday to Sunday 11am to 5pm,
Closed week prior to Christmas Day

admission: Weekends (Engines in
steam) Adults £3.80 OAPs £2.50
Children (5 - 15) £2.00. Weekdays
(Engines static) Adults £2.80 OAPs
£1.50 Children (5 -15) £1.00.

how to get there: The location is about 100 yards from the north side
of Kew Bridge. Look out for the tall Victorian tower. Parking is free in
the yard beside the entrance.

This Museum is devoted to the history of water supplies to London
and the pumping machinery is enormous. These engines have names
like Grand Junction 90 and Maudsley Engine. We went during the
week and the engines were not in action but if you go at weekends
many of the engines are in steam (this is the technical term for a
working engine) so do take children who are mad about steam engines
or machinery. The Museum is housed in a magnificent 19th century
pumping station.

There is a small café only open at the weekends which provides hot
and cold snacks, coffee, tea or soft drinks. There are many volunteer
helpers who are dedicated to the engines so it would not be difficult to
find someone to explain things to the children.

At the moment they do not have any special facilities for children like
workshops or quizes but are introducing such activities in the future.
There is a shop at the entrance to the museum which has the usual T-
Shirts, pens plus a good range of books.

THE LONDON MUSEUM

London Wall,
London EC2Y 5HN
tel: 0171 600 3699
age groups: 10 - 15
admission: Adults £4, OAPs &
Children £2.00
opening times: Monday to
Saturday 10am to 5.50pm,
Sunday 12 noon to 5.50pm,

how to get there: Underground - St. Paul's (Central Line).
Buses - 4, 56, 172.

The Museum of London traces the history of London and Londoners from prehistory to the present day. The Lord Mayor's wonderfully ornate coach is housed here. They have lots of events for children and in the holidays and half terms there are workshops for children. Be warned - it is a very large museum so try to do one small section or 'phone to find out what is going on.

THE LONDON PLANETARIUM

Marylebone Road, London
NW1
tel: 0171 935 6861
opening times: Monday to
Friday 9am to 5.30pm,
Saturday and Sunday 9am to
5.30pm
age group: 10 - 15
admission: Adults £5.85, OAPs
£4.50, Children £3.85

how to get there: Underground - Baker Street. Buses - 13, 30, 159.

This is an incredible experience and children, as adults are, are fascinated by space. The show takes place every 40 minutes. The Planetarium always seems to be busy and long queues form for both this and for Madame Tussaud's, especially in holiday times. Try to get here half an hour before a show begins so you have time to explore the interactive Planet Zone and Space Zone exhibition areas.

LONDON TOY AND MODEL MUSEUM

21-23 Craven Hill, London W2.
tel: 0171 706 8000
age group: 5 - 8
opening times: Monday to Saturday 10am to 5.30pm
admission: Adults £5.50, OAPs £3.50, Children £3.50
how to get there: Underground - Paddington or Lancaster Gate. Buses - 12, 94, 15, 23, 36

The London Toy & Model Museum

This is not a well advertised museum and in fact it is something of a discovery. You step back into an Edwardian nursery, so it is instructive and then there is the Whatever Next Gallery which gives you a glimpse into the future and shows you more modern toys not yet in the shops.

One of the most popular things for small visitors to do here is to ride on the miniature steam train in the garden - my six year old twins adored this. Try to go during the week when it is not at all crowded. There is a cafeteria which overlooks the garden.

LONDON TRANSPORT MUSEUM

Covent Garden, London WC2E 7BB
tel: 0171 565 7299 (recorded information)
0171 379 6344 (administration)
age group: 5 - 15
admission: Adults £4.95, OAPs £2.95, Children £2.95
opening times: 10am to 6pm every day except Fridays when it opens at 11am. Closed Dec 24th, 25th, 26th.
how to get there: Underground - Covent Garden Holborn, or Leicester Square. Buses - Strand or Aldwych 1, 4, 6, 9, 11, 13, 15, 23, 26, 68, 76, 77a, 91, 168, 171, 171a, 176, 188, 501, 505, 521

This is a beautifully laid out Museum run by London Transport and is suitable for all age groups but with a definite slant towards children.

Basically, you are learning the history of London Transport–of trams, buses and the Underground. You can see wonderful old trams, buses both horse drawn and from the modern day. Children can sit in most of them. We had a lovely guide who had experienced much change and was good at imparting his knowledge to my 8-year-old granddaughter.

The Museum seems to be very conscious that it should be a fun day out for all the family and there are many things for the children to push, pull, switch on and an action sheet which was much enjoyed and encouraged a greater awareness of the exhibits.

During the school holidays there is much more organised in the way of workshops, lectures and story telling but you should always phone to find out what is happening.

MADAME TUSSAUDS

Marylebone Road, NW1.
tel: 0171 935 6861

age group: 8 - 15
opening times: Monday to Friday 9am to 5.30pm, Saturday and Sunday 9am to 5.30pm
admission: Adults £9.75, OAPs £7.45, Children £6.60; for joint tickets to visit Madame Tussauds and the London Planetarium Adults £12, OAPs £9.25, Children £8.50
how to get there: underground - Baker Street. Buses: 13,30,159.

The most famous waxworks in the world, in 1997 it was Britain's top admission charging tourist attraction, consequently the queues seem to be endless so be sure to arrive early in the morning. It represents famous people both past and present, heroes, villains, well known politicians, The Royal Family and so on. Part of the appeal seems to be that people can meet the famous and be photographed with them.

Clever marketing taught Madame Tussauds to remove the ropes that once protected the wax figures so that people could touch them - so you can kiss Brad Pitt or strangle Saddam Hussein just as the mood takes you! You have the ghoulish chamber of horrors with many notorious murderers on show - my children especially enjoyed this aspect of Tussauds.

One of the best attractions here takes place at the end of the tour, where you take a journey through 400 years of London life in a replica of an old black London cab. There are catering facilities here as well as a gift shop.

MUSEUM OF THE MOVING IMAGE

South Bank,Waterloo, London SE11
tel: 0171 401 2636
age group: 5 - 15
opening times: Monday to Sunday 10am to 6pm
We have all adored this museum - I think one of the great things about it is there is so much participation involved here when you are

wandering around. Basically you are seeing the moving image from the very start commencing with optical toys and going through the cinema, television and on into the future with all its special effects. There is something here for all age groups from 5 onwards to enjoy, but the older they are the more children seem to get out of this museum. Allow the children two good hours here. I guarantee they will not be bored.

THE NATIONAL ARMY MUSEUM

Royal Hospital Road, London SW3 4HT
tel: 0171 730 0717
age group: 8 - 15
opening times: Monday to Sunday 10am to 5.30pm, Closed December 24th, 25th and 26th, January 1st, Good Friday and May Bank Holiday

admission: Free

how to get there: Underground - District and Circle line to Sloane Square. Buses - 11, 19, 22, 21 along King's Road, 137 to Pimlico Road, 239 stops directly outside the Museum

This Museum is centrally situated and immediately next door to the Royal Chelsea Hospital, so if you have children fascinated with the army they can combine the museum with seeing how the Chelsea Pensioners live in their magnificent Christopher Wren designed building.

I am not very interested in the Army but this museum is so well laid out and so informative I became totally absorbed in all it had to offer. There is a feast of famous paintings, colourful uniforms, and the story of soldiers' every day lives from the 15th century to the present day. I particularly enjoyed the description of the Battle of Waterloo.

There are many places to sit on your way around and a few areas where you watch a short video of something of interest; all welcome breaks for tired feet!

There is a café serving snacks and light lunches and a small but interesting gift shop.

NATIONAL MARITIME MUSEUM

Romney Road, Greenwich, London SE10 9EF
tel: 0181 858 4422
age group: 10 - 15
opening times: Daily 10am to 5pm except 25th & 26th December
admission: Adults: £5.00 OAPs £4.00 Children under 16 £2.50. Your ticket is valid for 1 year so do not lose it! It also includes entry to the Queen's House and the Old Royal Observatory
how to get there: Boat form Westminster, Charing Cross or Tower Bridge. Docklands Light Railway to Island Gardens then walk through foot tunnel. Train - to either Maze Hill or Grenwich Station.

Fascinating to see Britain's maritime heritage illustrated through things like model ships, paintings, uniforms and navigation and astronomy instruments. There is an area called the All Hands Gallery which is fun for both children and adults. For example, you can load cargo onto a boat so it doesn't list, experience the difficulty of undertaking a maritime job below water or send messages with flags to name just a few things. The boys loved this part of the museum.

Your ticket takes you into the Royal Observatory - another unique experience, and also the Queen's House which has been 'done up' in the last few years. It is the first Palladian Building in England built in 1638 and has a truly magnificent exterior.

NATURAL HISTORY MUSEUM

Cromwell Road, London SW7
tel: 0171 938 9123
age group: 6 - 15
opening times: Monday to Saturday
10am to 5.30pm, Sunday 11am to
5.30pm
admission: Adults £6, OAPs £3.20,
Children £3.

how to get there: Underground - South Kensington. Buses -14,30,74.
The great attraction here for the younger children is quite definitely the Dinosaur Exhibition. It was only put on for a short time but proved so successful that it is now a permanent fixture. This is housed in the Life Galleries and there are several more facets to this section, such as woods and animals. Children are well catered for with hands-on activity sheets which they can keep. The older child will find the Earth Galleries fascinating - one of the many experiences here is a simulated earthquake which takes place in a Japanese supermarket and is brilliantly staged. They have recently extended the Earth Galleries so you will find plenty to see and do here. Try to go on two separate occasions, Life Galleries on one visit and Earth Galleries on another.

POLLOCK'S TOY MUSEUM

1 Scala Street, London W1P 1LT
tel: 0171 636 3452
age groups: 5 - 15
opening times: 10am to 5pm daily except Sundays and Bank Holidays

admission: Adults £2.50 under 18's £1.00

How to get there: Underground - Goodge Street Northern Line, Buses - 10,24,29,73 to Goodge Street, Car - difficult to park

This is a unique toy shop with a museum on the first and second floors of two terraced houses which have been knocked into one. The whole idea started in 1856 as a theatrical warehouse and progressed into toy theatres which came from Germany with toys and dolls. Much of course has changed but the premises were only moved into in the late 1960s and the tradition of the toy theatre has remained. These are sold in the shop and are made from paper. I have never seen them anywhere else and I bought three theatres for the grand sum of £5.95 each for my granddaughters who had much pleasure assembling them.

The museum evolved when Marguerite Fawdry took over the shop in 1956. She had a small collection of toys which just continued to grow. By keeping to the theatrical theme it is a unique collection and by the very nature of the layout of the rooms has a charm all of its own.

Gay Wandron who manages the shop does the buying too and is keen to stock things that children can make. It is intriguing to see the more unusual items.

RAGGED SCHOOL MUSEUM

46-50 Copperfield Road, Bow, London E3 4RR
tel: 0181 980 6405
age group: 8 - 15
opening times: Wednesday - Thursday 10am - 5pm; First Sunday of each month 2pm - 5pm
admission: Free
how to get there: Underground - Mile End. Buses - D6, D7, 25, 277, 309

This East End Museum has a special focus on the work of Dr Barnardo and education in Victorian times. It is also developing as a museum about life in the East End.

The school was originally started as a free day school by Dr Barnardo in two Victorian warehouses. Ragged schools (so-called because of the state of the children) provided free education to the children of the poor.

The school room has been lovingly recreated, a pretty tough way of learning I would say. There are guides on hand, local volunteers, and visitors can understand what conditions at school and in the East End were like.

There are workshops during school holidays for children aged 7 and above on the days that they are open. Although we have not done any of these they sound most interesting. Entrance to the museum is free, as are the workshops, although numbers for the workshops are limited and are almost always full. Guided tours for adults are available for a small charge but contact the museum in advance.

ROCK CIRCUS

London Pavilion, Piccadilly Circus, London W1V 9LA
tel: 0171 734 7203
age group: 8 - 15
admission: Adults £7.95 O.A.P.'s and Students £6.95 Children under 16 £6

opening times Monday, Wednesday & Thursday 11am to 9pm, Tuesday 12noon to 9pm
how to get there: Underground - PIccadilly Circus or Leicester Square Buses - 3, 6, 9, 12, 13, 14, 15, 19, 23, 38, 53, 88.

The Rock Circus is part of Madame Tussauds' but the great thing is you don't seem to have to queue for so long!

It is well laid out and you must allow a good hour to walk round the wax exhibits. For the first part of the exhibition you walk around with headphones on and listen to 40 years of the history of Rock and Pop. As you stand in front of each exhibit you hear some of their music.

The latter part of the visit is the Rock Show, done in a specially designed revolving theatre again with 40 years of music shown on the screen and with animated lifesize wax figures made more exciting by the use of lasers and good lighting. The gift shop is full of fun pop memorabilia and the inevitable pop posters which can be purchased. Not a cheap outing, but exciting and fun.

ROYAL AIR FORCE MUSEUM

Grahams Park Way, London NW9
tel: 0181 205 2266
age group: 10 - 15.
admission: Adults £6.50 OAPs £4.90
Children £3.25
opening times: Monday to Sunday 10am to
6pm
how to get there: Underground - Northern
Line to Collindale (10 minutes walk).
Buses - 303

It is a bit of a trip but rewarding when you get there. Everything is well displayed in large exhibition halls and covers the history of aviation from its inception. To my grandsons the Battle of Britain Hall was the most interesting and in this we joined the guided tour which was well done by a really delightful RAF veteran. There is plenty of parking and the grounds are ideal for a picnic. There is a restaurant called "Wings" which I can highly recommend. Take grandsons to this museum and granddaughters if they are interested in aeroplanes.

THE SCIENCE MUSEUM

Exhibition Road, London SW7
tel: 0171 938 8008
age group: 3 - 15
opening times: Monday to Sunday 10am
to 6pm, Closed December 24th, 25th and
26th.
admission: Adults £9.50 Children £5.50
OAPs £5.50
how to get there: Underground - South
Kensington. Buses - 9, 9A, 10, 14, 49, 74,
C1.

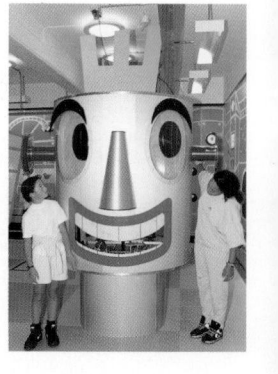

This is a wonderful museum for the enquiring mind, a place you can go back and back to so don't feel the need to take it all in one go. Allow one or two hours and choose what you are going to do. In the basement of the museum is the garden which is aimed at the 3 to 6 year olds as they can explore and discover in an exciting environment. They can build with giant Lego type bricks, watch water flowing from a huge bucket into a series of pots which can alter with drains and pumps. There is also a tool shed where children can experiment with materials and structures. Another area in the basement is called The Secret Life of the Home which is all about the labour saving devices for the home and again you have many hands-on exhibits. Finally in the basement you have 'Things' which is about how everything works and what it does. This is for the 7 to 11 year olds and for them it provides a real challenge presented in an appealing way.

On the ground floor you have the Exploration of Space which the older children will love. On the first floor is the Launch Pad which is a hands-on gallery with over 50 interactive exhibits aimed at all ages of children. There is a team of what they call Explainers dressed in green shirts who will help you to get more out of the visit. All my grandchildren adore this area of the museum.

On the third floor go to On Air aimed at the 7 to 15 year olds and here they have an ingenious computer which allows you to complete a 'mix' and hear what it sounds like. Here you will also find The Flight Lab, a hands-on gallery containing 20 or so interactive exhibits on how aircraft fly with 'The Explainers' on hand.

This museum is really so child friendly. There are three eating areas which are of a good standard and I was impressed with the seating all around the museum, but particularly around the childrens activity areas.

SHERLOCK HOLMES MUSEUM

221B Baker Street, London NW1
tel: 0171 935 8866
age group: 12 - 15
admission: Adults £5., OAPs £5, Children £3
opening times: Monday to Sunday 9.30am to 6pm
how to get there: Underground - Baker Street. Buses - 82, 113

This is a specialist museum so it is no good embarking on it unless your child has a reasonable knowledge of Sherlock Holmes and Dr. Watson and before the age of 12 these are probably not the books they will have read. Having said this, if you are lucky enough to have a child keen on Sherlock Holmes, this is a beautifully presented small museum.

Your first experience happens outside Baker Street tube station where Holmes is waiting for you armed with leaflets and instructions on how to get to 221B Baker Street. The house was purchased 10 years ago by an enthusiastic entrepreneurial older lady (also a Granny!!) and with loving care and attention to detail she has turned it into the home of Holmes and Watson, and presented exactly as described in the stories. You are greeted by a policeman at the front door and escorted around the small house by a Victorian maid. You can then round off the experience by having lunch or a cream tea at Mrs Hudson's next door. Your children can answer a questionnaire as they go round which does make them more observant and this is given to you by the maid as you enter.

SIR JOHN SOANE'S MUSEUM

13 Lincoln's Inn Fields, London WC2A 3PB
tel: 0171 430 0175
age group: 12 - 15
admission: Free
open times: Tuesday - Saturday 10am to 5pm; On first Tuesday of every month 6pm to 9pm
how to get there: Underground - Holborn

I just mention this small Museum because it was the home of Sir John Soane, the famous architect who designed the Bank of England. The house has some wonderful furniture and artifacts and you feel that Sir John still lives here.

It is not going to appeal to all children but older ones might just be interested to see how this well known architect lived in London. It takes approximately an hour to go round the Museum.

THE TATE GALLERY

Millbank, London SW1P 4RG
tel: 0171 887 8000
age group: all ages
admission: Free
opening times: Daily from 10.00am to 5.50pm. Closed December 24th, 25th & 26th
how to get there: Underground - Pimlico. Buses - 77A, 88, C10 all pass the door. 2, 36, 159, 567, stop nearby.
Cars: A few parking meters near the Gallery N.C.P. 2 minutes away.

This is one of my favourite London Galleries. Somehow it combines the old and the modern in a very sympathetic way and they are certainly children friendly. If you ask at the information desk for an activity sheet you will get interesting material (all free) which certainly stimulates the children's minds.

The Art Trolley is a clever idea which operates at the weekends and in the holidays and consists of a wide range of games, trails, puzzles and other fun activities for adults and children to do together. I hope this idea is adopted by other museums.

During the summer holidays there are special activities but it is advisable to telephone to ask for details.

The catering arrangements are good. If you want a meal in a beautiful room go to the Whistler Restaurant which has a mural painted by Rex Whistler in 1925. The food and ambience are first class but so are the prices! The adjoining cafeteria is also well done and reasonably priced.

The Tate gift shops we loved. Modern art posters sit alongside other unusual gifts and souvenirs.

THEATRE MUSEUM

Russell Street, Covent Garden, London WC2E 7PA
tel: 0171 836 7891

age group: 6 - 15
admission: Adults £3.50, OAPs & Children £2.00
opening times: 11am to 7pm Tuesday to Saturday
how to get there: Underground - Covent Garden, Leicester Square,

The Theatre Museum is part of the Victoria & Albert Museum and what a wonderful place it is for anyone interested in the theatre. It positively buzzes with activity.

The officials are child friendly and the day we were there we saw a theatrical make-up demonstration, a workshop for making masks and a costume workshop. The latter was particularly interesting as the children had the opportunity to try on costumes. There is a video

theatre with ongoing recordings of famous actors, which to me was very nostalgic.

There are guided tours lasting 20 to 30 minutes and for the older child this is excellent. As one would expect from a theatre museum, everything is theatrically displayed with movement and lighting.

Allow a good two hours here. There are no catering facilities or shops but you should find enough in Covent Garden itself to provide for all age groups.

THE VICTORIA & ALBERT MUSEUM

Cromwell Road, South Kensington, London SW7 2RL
tel: 0171 938 8500
age group: 10 - 15
admission: Adults £5, OAPs £3, Children under 17 Free
opening times: Monday 12noon to 5.45pm; Tuesday to Sunday 10am to 5.45pm everyone admitted free after 4.30pm
how to get there: Underground - South Kensington. Buses - 9, 9A, 10, 14, 74

I think I would describe the Victoria and Albert Museum as awesome but friendly. It certainly is some museum!

On arrival at the main entrance you find a large information desk manned by 12 knowledgeable volunteers. There is a short young persons tour of the ground floor of the gallery and this is best done with a visitors' information sheet.

Then there are organised gallery tours which are well constructed. I did one and loved it. This all comes under the umbrella of the V & A education programme. The day we went there were four different trails we could have chosen.

The catering is good here. They call it the New Restaurant although it has been open for several years, all self service with a lovely imaginative selection of hot and cold dishes. It is quite a long walk from the main entrance but there is plenty to see on the way. They also offer drinks and sandwiches in the courtyard gallery in the summer months when the weather is fine. It is known as the Pirelli Café and you can take your own sandwiches and sit here.

The V & A shop like everything else at the V & A is big. Much of the merchandise is reproduction antiques, particularly the jewellery but from the children's point of view there is little trivia for them to buy – I think something of a relief for those accompanying them.

Once again I have to say that only you know what your children will enjoy. All I can do is pass on to you my own opinions and experiences. The only problem could be that there's too much to choose from! Here are the things I have found to be fun for my family in the way of activities and sport.

THE B.B.C. EXPERIENCE (ADVANCE BOOKING ADVISED)

Broadcasting House, Portland Place, London W1A IAA
tel: 0870 60 30 304
age group: 10 - 15
admission: Adults £6.50 OAPs £5.50 Children (under 16) £4.50
opening times: (which can vary) Monday 1pm to 4.30pm, Tuesday to Sunday 10am to 4.30pm.
how to get there: Underground - Oxford Circus or Great Portland Street. Buses - Oxford Circus, walk down Portland Place.

My 15 year old Grandson, Tom Elliot, wrote this report:

On one of my many trips to London with my Grandmother, we decided to visit the B.B.C. Experience and see what happens inside Broadcasting House. When we arrived we met our tour guide who was informative and could answer any questions about the Marconi Radio and many of its first uses.

The museum was very hands-on, with many things to try out. We saw a film about how everything works in a radio studio and then went live to each station which was very enjoyable. We then went on to be part of the cast of a radio play and see a montage of photography and sound, outlining the part that the B.B.C. has played in history.

The last part of our tour was the best.

The Interactivity Centre enabled visitors to become a commentator on Gareth Southgate's penalty miss, host a weather show, and even be the editor for an episode of 'Eastenders'. It was very amusing seeing some of the end results. There was also a brilliant shop and café selling many pieces of memorabilia from the museum.

The whole tour took one hour and blended fun and interest very well. I thoroughly enjoyed it and would happily go again.

BRIDGEWATER POTTERY AND CAFÉ

735 Fulham Road, London SW6 5UL
tel: 0171 736 2157
age group: 5 - 15
opening times: phone in advance

This is a brilliant idea for helping the young to be creative and decorate their own individual piece of pottery. For children from the age of 5 upwards it's a fun experience. The Pottery Café is a large studio with tables and chairs where you sit to do your painting. You are asked to choose from a selection of cups, saucers, plates, bowls, teapots and jugs, etc., all undecorated and unglazed. You are then supplied with different colours of paint, brushes, sponges and enthusiastic staff show you and the children exactly what to do.

I took my three granddaughters, twins aged 6 1/2 and an 8 1/2 year old. They painted three small teapots and were kept amused for two hours. I picked the teapots up three days later, glazed and fired and they were so proud of the results. The teapots are now in pride of place in their parents' sitting room. Being creative does cause one to need sustenance and here you can have delicious cakes, tea, coffee and cold drinks which makes such a difference.

The cost of the outing depends on how many pieces you decide to decorate. You have to pay for whatever you are painting, plus a studio charge of £5 per person. My bill for the three children was £51, but what a great morning, with some going home presents to round it all off.

There are many other pottery studios opening up in London as we go to press such as:
Paint Your Own Pottery Cafe, The Chelsea Gardener, 123 Sydney Street, London SW3
Colour Me Mine, 168 - 170 Randolph Avenue, Maida Vale, London W9 1PE Tel: 0171 328 5577

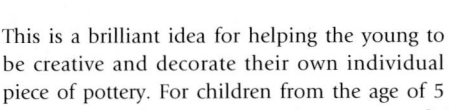

CAROL SINGING IN TRAFALGAR SQUARE

age group: all ages.
opening times: see press.
how to get there: Underground - Charing Cross. Buses - 3, 6, 11, 12, 13, 24, 53, 77A, 88, 159.

At the beginning of December, a very large Christmas Tree goes up in Trafalgar Square. This is a gift from the Norwegian Government in recognition of our help to them during the second World War. It always looks fantastic and various charitable organisations hold carol singing evenings round the tree. The atmosphere is magical and children of all ages love the experience. Watch the press for details.

CHESSINGTON WORLD OF ADVENTURE

Chessington, Surrey KT9 2NE
tel: 01372 729560 01372 727227 (recorded information)
age group: 4 - 15
admission: Adults £19.00 Children (4 - 14) £15.00 OAPs £8.50.

opening times: Mid March to November 1st seven days a week 10am to 5pm.
how to get there: By road. Situated on the A243 just 2 miles from both the A3 and M25 (Junctions 9 & 10). Free parking
Rail: 30 minutes from Waterloo.
Also rail services from Clapham Junction and Wimbledon to Chessington South which is a 10 minute walk from the main entrance. Buses - Local bus 71 Coach Flightline 777 from Victoria.

Although the price seems high it is value for money as you can have as many rides as you want (as well as shows and animal presentations) - so plan to spend a whole day here and preferably take another adult with you as it is hard work keeping an eye on the children as they go from ride to ride. All ages are well catered for. Some rides were far too frightening for me to go on but the older children seem to have no fear. Many of the rides are suitable for very small children.

There are plenty of places for food: McDonalds, Pizza Hut etc. - all fast food but just what the children want. From mid July to the end of August the opening times are extended until later in the evening on certain days. If you require further information do ring - they are most helpful on the telephone.

THE CUTTY SARK

King William Walk, Greenwich Pier SW10.
tel: 0181 858 3445
age group: 7 - 15
admission: Adults £3.50 Children (under 16) £2.50 OAPs £2.50
opening times: April to September Monday to Saturday 10am to 6pm and Sunday 12noon to 6pm. October to March Monday to Saturday 10am to 5pm & Sunday 12noon to 7pm.
how to get there: by boat from Westminster, Charing Cross, or Tower Piers. By train from Charing Cross to Maze Hill.

This is a marvellous tea clipper built in 1869 and now lying permanently in dry dock. This can be a fun focal point for your trip down the Thames to Greenwich - but don't forget it takes a long time to get there. (See Water Bus in section seven). The ship is fascinating, and it is incredible to see how the sailors survived the hazardous conditions on these clippers. Nearby is Gypsy Moth which was the yacht Sir Francis Chichester sailed single handed round the world in 1966. Boys and girls between 12 to 14 who are keen on sailing would particularly enjoy this day out.

COVENT GARDEN BUSKING

The Piazza, Covent Garden, London WC2
tel: 0171 836 9136
age group: 6 - 8, but variable.
how to get there: Underground - Covent Garden, Leicester Square.

The fruit market has moved to Nine Elms now, but there is still a great deal of interest with shops, stalls and cafés. Ring the number given for details of busking, or about what else might be going on. I find that small children are fascinated by the activity of some buskers and many of them, specially on a Saturday morning, are geared to the young. I found on a couple of occasions my most outgoing grandchild was up there with the buskers the moment they asked for a small volunteer. This entertainment is free unless you get caught in the shops in the area!

FOOTBALL CLUBS

age group: 5 - 14

My grandsons are staunch supporters of Chelsea so this is the only club I am familiar with but I have given the addresses of the other Premier League clubs in London and they offer some of the same facilities as Chelsea.

You must phone for details but besides the matches, which may not be ideal for the smaller children, the other facilities for football crazy youngsters are perfect. They can go on organised tours around the ground, meet some of their pin up heros or visit the souvenir gift shops. You can even give a childrens party at the ground.

In the summer of 1997, Chelsea opened an enormous Megastore, I am told it is the biggest in the country and there is nothing it seems that you cannot buy - of course everything has the Chelsea colours and logo on it: T shirts, trousers, badges, wallpaper, curtain material, baby clothes, duvet covers it just seems endless. It is on two floors and boasts 14 check out points. You can even hold the Cup and be photographed doing so for the pricey sum of £29.99 (my grandchildren were thrilled to do this). Many of the other London clubs also have excellent club stores.

Arsenal F.C. Avenell Road N5 tel: 0171 704 4000
Charlton Athletic F.C. The Valley, Foyd Road SE7 tel: 0181 333 4000
Chelsea F.C. Stamford Bridge Ground SW6 tel: 0171 385 5545
Tottenhasm Hotspur F.C. 748 High Road N17 tel:0181 386 5000
West Ham United F.C. Green Street E13 tel: 0181 548 2748

Wimbledon F.C. Selhurst Park Stadium, Whitehorse Lane SE25 tel: 0181 544 0330

GREAT THORPE PARK

Staines Road, Chertsey, Surrey KT16 8PN
tel: 01932 569393
age group: 4 - 15
admission: Adults £16.50 Children under 14 (and taller than 1 metre) £13.00 OAPs £13.00. Children under 1 metre tall are free.
opening times: Third week in March until end October 9.30am to 6pm (I would advise you to check times by telephoning in advance as they may vary slightly) Please ring the info line for opening dates & times on 01932 562633
how to get there: Train from Waterloo to Staines takes approximately 15 minutes. Then a short bus ride to Thorpe Park
By car: follow the M25, take junction 11 or 13 & follow the A320 to Thorpe Park. Good parking facilities on site.

This is a great theme park. It has been open for 19 years and was one of the first and is one of the best in terms of layout and organisation. The entrance fee includes all rides and there is a big emphasis on water. We loved the big waterslide where they photograph you coming down.
There are plenty of eating places (nine in total) so everyone should be able to find something they like. All ages are well catered for here but as with all big theme parks it is not a bad idea to have two adults in charge.

HMS BELFAST

Morgan's Lane, off Tooley Street, London SE1
tel: 0171 940 6300
age group: 10 - 15
admission: Adults £4.70 Children £2.40 OAPs £3.60
opening times: March - October Monday to Sunday 10am to 6pm, November to February Monday to Sunday 10am to 5pm.

how to get there: Underground - London Bridge or Tower Hill. Buses -

10, 44, 48, 70, 133. Water Bus to London Bridge Pier

This is an old naval ship which played an important part in the 2nd World War. It is moored near the Tower of London and has been kept very much as it was during its years of service. Don't take young children to this. It is very much for children between the ages of 10 and 14 - it takes quite a long time to view it all and there are a lot of steps. It can be combined with a trip to the London Dungeons, also in Tooley Street.

Hyde Park Riding Stables

63 Bathurst Mews, Lancaster Gate, London W1
tel: 0171 723 2813
age group-: 5 - 15
admission: £25 per hour payable in advance. No refund on cancellation, 10 hour course £200.00
how to get there: Underground - Lancaster Gate, Marble Arch. Buses - 12, 94
This is a well organised, happy riding school and they take good care

of your child. There are two riding arenas in Hyde Park. One is opposite the Knightsbridge Barracks and a smaller one is off North Carriage Drive. The beginners are always on leading reins until they are able to ride in the arenas.

If you have a young person who is having withdrawal symptoms having left a pony behind in the country, it is a great place to offer some comfort. They will take children from the age of 5.

Go Karting - Playscape Pro Racing Ltd

Heston Road, Off Battersea Bridge, London SW11
tel: 0171 801 0110
age group: 8 - 15
opening times: Monday to Friday 10am to 5.30pm Saturday and Sunday 10am to 2am.
how to get there: Underground - Sloane Square, then take Bus 19 to Heston Road.
I was so popular when I discovered this. Give young boys and some

young girls an engine, four wheels and a racing track and you have sent them to heaven! The young attendants are so helpful and understanding in explaining how to drive the Karts, also the attention to safety is impressive. It is an expensive outing - I only let them have half an hour, but it takes time to get them all kitted up with overalls and helmets and at the end there is a machine for drinks and you can watch other folk going round the track. So allow a good hour for this outing. Every 4th Saturday they have a teach-in with instruction and practice. I have only been once with my grandsons but they loved it.

THE GREAT BALLOON EXPERIENCE

Spring Gardens, Vauxhall Bridge, London SE11 5HF
tel: 0345 023842, 24 hr info line
age group: 6 - 15
admission charges: Adults £12; Children under 12 £7.50, No concessions for OAPs
opening times: Monday to Saturday 10am to dusk, Friday, Saturday & Sunday night flights until midnight depending on weather conditions
how to get there: Underground: Vauxhall (100 metres from the underground)

Once over Vauxhall Bridge it is not difficult to spot the Balloon. Big Bob as it is known is the largest helium filled gas balloon in the world, operated by a winch with electric and hydraulic motors. It ascends to a great height, dependent somewhat on weather conditions. It is extremely safe having passed rigorous safety regulations and the views from the gondola under the balloon are breathtaking as you look down the Thames towards the Houses of Parliament.

My only big criticism was the cost which I felt was rather high, to coin a phrase, for 15 minutes up in the air, especially as there are no concessions for OAPs. Flights go every 15 minutes and will take 28 people. Try not to take a car as it's difficult to park nearby.

KENWOOD HOUSE

Hampstead Lane, London NW3 7TR
tel: 0181 348 1286
age group 10 -15
admission: Free
opening times: April 1st to September 30th 10am to 6pm , October 1st to October 31st 10am to 5pm , November 2nd to March 31st 10am to 4pm
how to get there: Buses - 210, Underground - Archway and Golders Green on the Northern Line then take the 210 bus to the door.

We went on one of those perfect English summer days and were not at all disappointed with what we found. Kenwood is part of English Heritage and has been lovingly restored. They have a fine collection of paintings given to the nation and 112 acres of landscaped grounds with outstanding views of London as the position of the house is high. Robert Adam, the well-known architect of the 18th century, was responsible for remodelling the house.

Children are well catered for here but I would suggest Kenwood is not suitable for those younger than 10 years. Children are supplied with activity sheets which include questionnaires they can fill in as they wander around and learn about the house.

The café is great, we had lunch there. It is possible to get anything from a full blown hot meal to a light snack and it is all self service. There is a terrace outside the café where you can sit, drink and eat overlooking the gardens.

Do not overlook picnics, the grounds are so lovely and it also makes the trip a less expensive excursion–unless you are tempted into the two gift shops, both of which I purchased from!

In the summer months Kenwood puts on lakeside concerts and firework displays. Phone to enquire what is going on and when.

KEW GARDENS

Kew, Richmond, Surrey TW9 3AB
age groups: all
telephone: 0181 940 1171 (recorded information), 0181 332 5000
admission: Adults £5.00 OAPs £3.50 Children (5 - 16) £2.50 Children under 5 free
how to get there: Underground - District Line to Kew. Buses - take a bus to Hammersmith then change to the 391 from Hammersmith to Kew.

I should emphasise that at Kew Gardens you find the Royal Botanical Gardens - perhaps one of the most famous of its type in the world. Among the many adults, 60,000 children a year visit Kew Gardens to enjoy the sight and scents in its 300 acres - four of them under glass - which contain the largest collection of plant species in the world. Even in winter a visit is full of fascination as the Palm House displays tropical plants from around the globe, including coffee, banana, and giant bamboo which can grow up to a metre a day. In the exhibition "Plants & People" you see man's use of plants and the Evolution House takes you on a journey through 350 hundred million years of plant life. The Princess of Wales Conservatory contains ten climatic zones - from steamy rain forest, to arid desert. There are two art galleries, a visitor centre, two gift shops and a restaurant but the Gardens are a wonderful place to picnic. If you have a child fascinated by plants and gardening this is fantastic.

It is also a lovely place to picnic, with wide open spaces but it is not a municipal park.

KENSINGTON GARDENS

W2.
tel: 0171 298 2100
age group: 3 - 8
opening times: Monday to Sunday dawn to dusk.
how to get there: Underground - Bayswater, Lancaster Gate, High Street Kensington. Buses - 12, 94

A lovely day if the children have pent up energy, so maybe reinforced with a picnic, you set off for an hour or two in Kensington Gardens. here you have to use your imagination and being a great lover of Peter Pan I don't find this difficult! Try to get a picture of Peter Pan in Kensington Gardens. The trees in Arthur Rackham's illustrations for the book are easy to identify and children are intrigued to try and find Peter Pan in the trees and look for the famous statue. This unfortunately is quite a long walk into the park but beautiful to look at and you can make this the focal point for a picnic. There is also the Round Pond (remember to take bread for the ducks and geese) and if you go at weekends you'll see many model boat enthusiasts radio-controlling their boats on the pond.

My grandchildren have all loved the beautiful walks not for the plants and flowers which I so much appreciate but for the numerous squirrels and pigeons which come and literally eat out of your hands.

LEGOLAND

Windsor Park, Berkshire.
tel: 0990 04 04 04
age groups: 3 - 12
admission : Adults £16.50 OAPs £10.50 Children (over 3) £13.50
opening times: 14 March to 1 November 10am to 6pm Mid July to end of August 10.00am to 8.00pm
how to get there: Ring the above number for public transport or coach trip ideas. You can buy tickets at either Waterloo or Paddington stations for an all-inclusive package (Train fare, transfer and admittance to Legoland), or go by car. 2 miles from Windsor town centre on the B3022 Bracknell/Ascot Road.

What a wonderful day I had with my twin grand daughters. I just could find no fault with Legoland.

There are limits to the numbers that can be accomodated so there's a free advance booking service which could avoid dissapointment particularly at busy times such as weekends and school holidays. Allow enough time for the tickets to be mailed to you so you can fast track ticket booths.

This is a copy of the celebrated Legoland in Denmark and every detail has been attended to. If you go outside the rush hour it will take approximately three quarters of an hour in the car to reach from the centre of London. It is a delight to be able to say that the whole area is carefully and tastefully landscaped and colour is the main ingredient with everything being built in primary colours.

There are so many things for the children to do such as a fairground with a horse carousel and miniature helicopters, a circus where the children act with actors (mine adored this), but the most popular thing of all is the driving school with traffic lights, roundabout and pedestrian crossings. The catering arrangements are excellent, plenty of them, with suitable food for both children and grown ups - or you can take a picnic and choose an umbrella table and seats to enjoy it at. There are really helpful attendants every where - this is a full, full day out. You and your children will come back happy and exhausted.

A new attraction is Castle Land which features the Dragon Knight's Castle, containing the roller-coaster ride called the Dragon. During the ride you travel through scenes of animated Lego models and fly through the treetops as the car increases in speed. For hands on experience for over 9's, there is a technology workshop, the Lego Mindstorm Centre, where players create their own sporting robot and programme it to score as many goals as possible on a specially designed sports pitch.

Legoland organise special event days such as King for a Day and Pirate Day, so call to find out what's going on. Facilities include the hire of wheelchairs and pushchairs and 'Lost Parents' meeting points.

B.F.G. *Legoland was founded in 1932 in Denmark and is still owned and run by the Kirk Christien family. Origionally, Ole Kirk Christien started making wooden toys in his small workshop in 1932. Two years later he invented the name Lego for his toys. This is a contraction of the Danish words 'let godt', meaning 'play well'. He later discovered that Lego also means 'I put together' or 'I assemble' in Latin. Legoland opened in Denmark in 1968 and in Windsor in 1996.*

LONDON AQUARIUM

County Hall, Westminster Bridge
Road, London SE1.
tel: 0171 967 8000
age group: 5 - 15
admission: Adults £7.00 OAPs
£6.00 Children (3-14) £5.00
opening times: Monday to Sunday
10am to 6pm Bank Holidays
9.30am to 7.30pm
how to get there: Underground - Westminster

This is the first large aquarium in London and is housed in the Old Country Hall, a great location. Everything is magnificently displayed from small tanks with dazzling colourful fish to enormous tanks holding a million litres of water displaying Sharks, Stingers, Groupers to name but a few, but to for me the highlight comes at the end where there is a touch pool and you are able to touch and stroke the very friendly rays. I find one to one and a half hours is about the right length of time to stay here.

Almost next door to the Aquarium is a smaller version or Segaworld which has been opened recently and there is also a good café where you can sit outside and watch the river flow by.

THE LONDON DUNGEON

Tooley Street, London SE1
tel: 0171 403 7221
age group: 8 -15
opening times: April - September Monday to
Saturday 10am to 6.30pm
how to get there: Underground - London
Bridge. Buses - 10, 44, 48, 70, 133.

This is horrible, but what a winner! After Madame Tussaud's this must be one of the top tourist attractions in London for children. They have recreated the horrors of torture and life in the dungeons in bygone days. You can witness an execution and walk the streets where Jack the Ripper carried out his horrendous murders. Children have a fascination for this sort of thing, but be careful if they are easily frightened – you don't want them up all night with nightmares. I'm sure you won't be popular with their parents if they have a sleepless night!

THE LORD MAYOR'S SHOW

City of London
telephone 0171 222 1234 for information about the show.
age group: all
commences 11am Sunday, first Sunday in November

The Lord Mayor's show is one of Britain's greatest traditional ceremonies and takes place every year at the beginning of November in the City of London.

It is a spectacle for all ages. The procession is nearly three miles in length with the focal point being the Lord Mayor in his magnificent gold coach being taken through the city to the Royal Courts of Justice

where he is 'sworn in' for his year's term of office. There are over 65 floats and 20 marching bands and the day ends at 5.00pm with a sensational firework display. This is started from a barge between Blackfriars and Waterloo Bridge. This is a perfect family day out, crowded but great fun!

QUEENS ICE SKATING RINK

17 Queensway, London W2 4QP
tel: 0171 229 0172
age group: 7 - 15
admission charges: Monday to Friday sessions 10 - 12 £4; 12 - 2 £6; 2 - 5 £6; 5 0 7 £5; 8 - 10 on Monday, Tuesday and Thursday £6; 8 - 10 on Wednesday £5; 8 - 11 on Fridays only £6.50, Saturday and Sunday sessions 10 - 12, 12 - 2, 2 - 5, 5 - 7 £6; 8 - 10 £5
All the above prices include skate hire.
Open Monday -Sunday sessions 10am to 2pm, 12noon to 2pm , 2pm to 5pm, 5pm to7pm, 8pm to 10pm (till 11pm on Fridays only)
how to get there: Underground - Bayswater or Queensway
Buses - Any going down Bayswater Road - get off at Queensway

This is a well established ice rink in Central London and we have had many fun sessions here.

If you are not a skating Grandmother (and I am not!) it does mean you have to stand and watch so be warned, wrap up well.

When they have finished skating there is an area with computer games and you can sit comfortably and watch them with a cup of coffee.

Before you go on this expedition it is advisable to phone and check the times that the rink is available. You do not need to own your own boots and skates as they can be hired from the rink.

ROSS NYE'S RIDING STABLES

8 Bathurst Mews, London W2
tel: 0171 262 3791
admission charges: £25 per hour
opening times: Tuesday to Sundays 7am to 11am, 2pm to 6pm

how to get there: Underground - Lancaster Gate and Marble Arch, Buses - 12 & 94

A riding school with 16 horses, all ages welcome from 5 upwards. They work in conjunction with Hyde Park Riding Stables and have excellent facilities for the horses and take great care of the little ones, insisting on leading reins.

THE ROYAL MEWS

Buckingham Palace Road, London SW1
tel: 0171 799 2331
age group: 7 - 14
admission charges: Adults £4 OAPs £3 Children under 17 £2
opening times: All year - Tuesday, Wednesday, Thursday 12noon to 4pm last admission 3.30pm. Between 3rd August and 1st October - Monday, Tuesday, Wednesday, Thursday 10am to 4.30pm last admission 4.30pm

This is one of the finest working stables in existence and a lovely outing for children addicted to horses.

It takes about an hour to explore The Mews fully. The horses are magnificently stabled in tiled stalls with masses of well polished brass everywhere. I think I was most impressed with the tack room, where everything just gleams at you–the hours that must go into the cleaning!

The State Carriages are also housed here including the unique Gold State Coach used for the Queen's Coronation in 1953 and again on the 25th anniversary of her ascension to the throne. This Coach takes 8 horses to pull it which gives you some idea of the weight. This is a unique way for children to see a working department of the Royal Household and to feel they have had a look behind the scenes, so to speak, of Buckingham Palace.

Do not arrive here at 3.31pm because they really do mean it when they say last admissions are at 3.30pm!

ROYAL TOURNAMENT

Earls Court Exhibition Centre, Warwick Road, London SW5
tel: 0171 233 0330
age group: 10 - 15
opening times: see press or 'phone.
how to get there: Underground - Earl's Court. Buses - 31, 74, C1, C3

This event is held from the middle to the end of July at Earl's Court and is a great show especially for those interested in the Forces. It consists of an impressive military spectacle with all the combined services taking part. It is good to get there an hour or so before it starts as there are some interesting interactive stands promoting the Army, Navy and Air Force. My grandchildren always seem to come out bedecked with badges and clutching loads of leaflets.

SEGAWORLD - TROCADERO

Piccadilly Circus, London W1
tel: 0171 734 2777
age group: 8 - 15
admission: Free
opening times: Sunday to
Thursday 10.00am to 12.00
midnight, Friday & Saturday
10.00 am to 1.00am

I think of all the treats this has to be the best - not for you but for them. It is a theme park, the world's largest indoor entertainment park, in the centre of London, with seven dramatic rides such as a virtual reality space mission. Each ride lasts up to 7 minutes and cost £2 or £3. There are six zone areas where you can play all kinds of video games. Allow them three hours here and feel quite saintly when they have finished. I give mine a certain amount of money each at the start of the session. The best value is to purchase a multi-ride ticket which includes 4 rides and costs £7.90, a saving of £4.00. Alternately you can buy a family ticket which costs £14.90 and includes 8 ride tickets to share around. There are over 400 video games, all the very latest and interactive from Sega Rally II to Rapid River which vary in cost from 20p to £2.00. Be prepared for an expensive three hours. This can be combined with eating out in Leicester Square or a visit to Tower Records and all the many souvenir shops on the ground floor and basement of Segaworld.

THE SERPENTINE

Hyde Park, London W1.
age group: 8 - 15

This area of Hyde Park has many interesting things to do in the summer months. You can take a rowing boat or pedalo out on Lake Serpentine. Roller blading while it is so fashionable at the moment has a whole area more or less cordoned off for it. In fact it is possible to get someone to teach your children to do this sport. I love watching here, there are plenty of seats and it can be very amusing to watch and see how skilled some of the top bladers are.

There is a good café with a terrace on to the lake, so this can be a rewarding afternoon for the 8 to 15 age group.

SYON PARK

Brentford, Middlesex TW8 8JF
tel: 0181 847 0976
age group: 3 - 8
1.Snakes & Ladders
2.The Butterfly House
3.The Aquatic Experience
opening times: Monday to Sunday 10am to 6pm

This can provide a whole day out for the younger children as you have three venues in one location, plus the park to picnic in. It is better if you have a car to get there as you have to change from train to bus if you are taking public transport and it involves too much walking for the young. It is only 8 miles west along the A4 out of London from Marble Arch.

Snakes & Ladders is an enormous indoor adventure playground, brilliantly constructed and a serious place for the young to let off steam. It has a massive three tier play frame built to R.O.S.P.A. standards.

The afternoon we went was busy with young mothers with pushchairs and toddlers and children up to about seven, not another Granny in sight! My three granddaughters loved the climbing frame and we then went on to the other two smaller attractions. The Butterfly House, interesting here to see the many butterflies flying around everywhere and the Aquatic Experience where fish and reptiles take centre stage. Both areas are small and we only spent a total of half an hour here.

There are catering facilities but it was a fine day so I was delighted we had brought a picnic which we consumed in Syon Park. This is beautifully laid out and my granddaughters loved the many peacocks strutting around the gardens.

TOP OF ST PAUL'S

St Paul's Cathedral, Ludgate Hill, London EC4
age group: over 6
opening times: Monday to Saturday 9am to 4.30pm
how to get there: Underground - St. Paul's. Buses - 6, 9, 11, 22, 25.

A great fun thing to do with energetic youngsters. You climb up 627 steps to one of the best views of the City of London. I personally have only done this twice and it nearly killed me but my young companions adore it. At the same time try and combine it with the beauty and splendour of St. Paul's (not nearly as popular!).

B.F.G. St. Paul's Cathedral was designed by Sir Christopher Wren and was built after the Great Fire of London.

TWICKENHAM: RUGBY UNION

Whitton Road, Twickenham
tel: 0181 892 8161 phone or see press for details of matches.

age group: 10 - 15
how to get there: by car on the A3 via Micham

If you have rugby mad grandchildren, they might want to watch a match on this holy of holies ground. You must get tickets beforehand which will be an effort, but this will be well rewarded.

THE TWICKENHAM EXPERIENCE & MUSEUM

Rugby Football Union, Whitton Road, Twickenham, TW1 1DZ
tel: 0181 892 2000
admission: Museum only. £2.50 Adults, £1.50 OAPs & Children
Twickenham Experience: same as museum. Tour price: £4.00 Adults, £2.50 OAPs & Children.
Open: Tuesday to Saturday 10.30am to 5pm (last admission 4.30pm)
Open Bank Holidays, Sunday: 2pm to 5pm, On match days: 11am to one hour before kick off to match ticket holders only, Closed: Mondays, Christmas Day, Boxing Day, Good Friday.
how to get there: BR Waterloo to Twickenham and then 10 minutes

walk to the ground. Buses - the 281 opposite Twickenham Station.

Having two keen young rugby players on my hands for a couple of days in the summer holidays made a trip to Twickenham a must.

We drove from central London, following the signs for the M3 which took just over half an hour. We went on the 10.30am tour which took 1 1/2 hours and we thoroughly enjoyed the whole thing. The guides are retired rugby enthusiasts. The gentleman who guided us had been President of the Club and there was nothing he did not know about the game or the ground. We were taken everywhere, into the stands, onto the pitch, changing rooms, Royal box and VIP areas. The history of rugby was explained by our guide who made everything amusing and instructive so by the time we had finished we were able to enjoy the Museum with more understanding.

The Museum has been brilliantly done. It is large but skillfully lit with good video footage and films and some clever room sets.

There is an excellent restaurant where you can have lunch with a selection of hot & cold dishes, coffee, tea and snacks, all reasonably priced. It is also possible to have a children's party in the restaurant and then be taken on the tour.

This must have been be one of our best outings but only take boys who are keen on rugby and don't take them at too young an age as it is a long day out.

THE UNDERGROUND

opening times: Monday to Saturday 5.30am to 12midnight, Sunday 7.30am to 11.30pm
age group: 3 - 6
how to get there: find an Underground map!

I know you are going to say what a dirty place to take children, but let the children participate in the experience, putting the money in to get the ticket, putting the ticket into the gates, the thrill of them opening and then the waiting for the train. If you have time to wait, show them where they are on the large map on the wall, get a bar of chocolate from one of the machines which are on many platforms. Soon you will start to see the Underground in a different light! Cross from one platform to another, just go two stops and then come back. All of my grandchildren have enjoyed spending an hour or two on the Underground and this time will be very helpful to them later on when they are older. But do avoid the rush hours!

B.F.G. *The first underground city transport system was opened in London in 1863.*

WESTMINSTER ABBEY BRASS RUBBINGS

Deans Yard, London SW1
age group: 8 - 14
admission: Free
opening times: Monday to Saturday 9am to 5pm, Closed on Sunday
how to get there: Underground - Westminster on the District Line
Buses - 3, 11, 12, 24, 77A, 211

The brass rubbing centre is situated in the Cloisters of Westminster Abbey. It was started in 1976 the first of many such centres now open all around the world.

We did this in the summer school holidays, perhaps the busiest time, so do go early in the morning to avoid being frustrated. The day we went there were a lot of elderly American tourists who were loving the whole experience. My grandsons chose to create large knights in all their armoury, The cost was £5.50 per rubbing, the smaller ones are less. They now have their rubbings pinned up alongside their Chelsea Football Club heroes and the odd pin up girl, the usual and more unusual assortment favoured by young boys!

This visit can be combined with Westminster Abbey–here you are charged OAPs £3, Adults £5 and Children between the ages of 11 and 18, £2.

There is a great deal to see in the Abbey but only take them if they are going to be really interested. We did a brief visit after we had done the rubbings and they had become more interested in the monumental brasses.

Brass rubbings can also be done at two other London churches:-

All Hallow-by-the-Tower

Byward Street, London EC3
tel: 0171 481 2928
admission: Free, but charges for rubbings
opening times: Monday to Saturday 10am to 4.30pm, Sunday 1pm to 4.30pm
how to get there: Underground - Tower Hill. Buses - 15, 100

St Martin-in-the-Fields

The Crypt, Trafalgar Square, London WC2
tel: 0171 930 9306
admission: Free, but charges for rubbings
how to get there: Underground - Charing Cross, Embankment. Buses - 9, 11, 24, 29, 176

Wimbledon Lawn Tennis Museum

Church Road, Wimbledon, London SW19
tel: 0181 946 6131
admission: Adults £3.00, Children under 16 & OAPs £2.00.
opening times: Tuesday to Saturday 10am to 5.00pm, Sundays 2pm to 5pm. Bank Holiday Mondays from Easter to September. Only open to those visiting the tournament during the Championships.
how to get there: Underground - Southfields on District Line (15 minutes walk) Rail: Wimbledon from Waterloo (25 minute walk) Bus: 93,39,200. Car: the best way and excellent free parking.

Not an easy place to get to by anything other than a car but the Museum is very worthwhile once you get there, in fact, I would say outstanding. There is so much to see and you learn about croquet, real tennis, the first lawnmower–to name just a few things that you might not be expecting. We loved the various exciting matches which have been put on video and the quiz and databanks are good for promoting interest in the game. There are authentic Edwardian and pre war room sets which we loved and it is interesting to see the famous Centre Court. There is no tour of the grounds like at Twickenham, Wembley and other famous sports grounds which is a shame as it would help to bring the place alive. There is an attractive café here which is reasonably priced and offers good home-made food. There is a small but well stocked shop at the Museum - no rubbish and everything with a tennis theme.

LONDON ZOO

Regent's Park, London NW1
tel: 0171 722 3333
age group: 3 - 8
admission: Adults £8.50, OAPs £7.50, Children (4 - 14) £6.00
opening times: March - October Monday to Sunday 10am to 5.30pm, November - February Monday to Sunday 10am to 4pm. Closed on Christmas Day.
how to get there: Underground to Baker Street, Regent's Park or Camden Town, then 274 bus. Buses - 274 from Marble Arch or Baker Street, 3 or 53 from Regent Street to Gloucester Gate, or C2 from Oxford Circus.

© London Zoo

London Zoo never fails to provide a good day out, but don't forget to find out about special prices for children and even OAPs! Half a day might be long enough as children's attention span is not always as long as ours. If you go by car, it's quite a walk from any of the car parks to the zoo so remember push chairs for the smaller ones. We always try to start with the elephants and the monkeys. Pick up a Daily Events Guide at the main gate for a list of special activities including feeding times and animal rides (seasonal). The cafeteria is quite good here if you haven't made a picnic and there seems to be an ice cream booth on every corner which can be a menace!

London is full of interest, as you can tell by the number of tourists who visit it, but I must repeat that only you can decide what will be of interest to the children you are going to entertain. Obviously their ages will be important when you are considering where to take them and what to do with them, but also remember to find out what their pet subjects are so their time with you is a real success. Anyway, to help you make up your mind, here is a taste of the monuments, palaces and other buildings that you can consider showing them - perhaps if they are very young only from the outside, or alternatively from the top of a London bus, or even occasionally from a London taxi, which is a fun experience in itself.

ALBERT MEMORIAL

Prince's Gate, Kensington Gore, London SW7
tel: 0171 225 1059
age group: 3 - 14
opening times: 10am to 6pm.
how to get there: Underground - Knightsbridge, South Kensington. Buses - 9, 52, 73.

On a nice day you might think of walking in Kensington Gardens, looking at the outside of the Royal Albert Hall, the statue of Peter Pan, or Kensington Palace - which sadly, because of Princess Diana's death, many children have heard about. Ring the Albert Memorial Visitor Centre to find out what the young might enjoy seeing there, such as the "jewels" on the orb.

B.F.G. *The private gardens of Kensington Palace were opened in 1728 and were opened to the public by Queen Victoria.*

BATTERSEA PARK

Albert Bridge Road, London SW11
tel: 0181 871 7530
age group: All ages
admission: Free except for Zoo
opening times: 8am to dusk
how to get there: Underground - Sloane Square District & Circle lines
Car - Either Albert Bridge Road, Prince of Wales Drive, Queen's Circus

or Queenstown Road. Buses - 19, 39, 44, 45, 49, 137, 170

Situated south of the river between the Albert and Chelsea Bridges Battersea Park can be a day out for all age groups. There is so much to see and do here.

Tennis courts can be hired on an hourly basis (£3.20 per hour, £4.30 after 6pm)

Rowing boats are also for hire at £3.20 per hour. Cricket takes place at weekends and children sometimes find this fun to watch.

Roller blading has its own designated area within the park.

The old Victorian pump house has recently been restored and the interior opened as an art gallery. There is also a small shop and information centre.

The adventure playground provides a variety of both outdoor and indoor activities for children aged 5 to 16 and consists of climbing structures, slides, swings etc and indoors a craft centre and workshops. They open from Tuesday to Friday at 3.30pm and at weekends and over the school holidays at 11am onwards but do make a phone call on 0181 871 6374 to find out what is currently going on. There is also attached to the playground a One O'Clock Centre which is a good place for the under 5's to play. This is open on Monday to Friday from 1pm to 4pm.

Each year there are special events in the park. When we went there was a fun fair in full swing so I was very popular! Every summer there is a Teddy Bear's picnic. The circus also comes to the park and live jazz is played in the evening around the lake during the summer months.

There is a café by the lake serving hot dogs, hamburgers, chips and ice-cream but I have found that a picnic works best in the park.

I use Battersea Park a great deal with my younger grandchildren for there always seems to be a variety of things to do. The parking is excellent and it is so central. I would strongly recommend that you telephone the Park Office who are very helpful in order to find out what is going on.

BATTERSEA PARK CHILDRENS ZOO

Battersea Park, London SW11
tel: 0181 871 7540
age group: 3 upwards
admission: Adults £1.20 Children & OAPs 60p
opening times: Easter until end September 10am to 5pm daily.
October to Easter 11am to 3pm on Saturdays and Sundays only.
how to get there: The Zoo is on the South Bank between Albert and
Chelsea Bridges. Buses - 19, 44, 49, 137, 249, 319, 344, 345
Underground - Sloane Square, District & Circle line (20 minutes walk
at least) Car: excellent car parking in pay & display Monday to Friday
30p per hour Saturday & Sunday 50p per hour.

The Zoo is compact and small children do not have time to get bored
as everything is so concentrated, but a pushchair as ever may be useful.
There are birds, fish, tortoises, pot bellied pigs, a few snakes and
monkeys. The whole area is in 5 acres. Pony rides are available during
the summer months.

Children's birthday parties are quite a feature here but please contact
the Zoo Events Office on 0181 871 7540 for more specific
information.

BUCKINGHAM PALACE

The Mall, London SW1
tel: 0171 839 1377
age group: 10 - 15
admission: Adults £9.50
OAPs £5.00 & Children
under 17
opening times: Open every
day from August 6th to
October 4th 9.30am to
4.30pm , last entry 4.30pm

how to get there: Underground - Green Park, Victoria, St James's Park

Buses - 11, 16, 24, 52, 73 or on foot from Trafalgar Square which allows a pleasant walk up the Mall.

In my opinion this is a visit for the older child, certainly over 10. At this age your grandchildren will appreciate the grandeur of the palace. King George III bought Buckingham House from the Duke Of Buckingham in 1762 and moved there with his young wife Queen Charlotte. King George IV, who acceded to the throne in 1820, commissioned the architect John Nash to extend the building but died before the work was completed. In 1837 the 19 year old Queen Victoria moved in three weeks after her accession. Now an official residence of Queen Elizabeth, her personal standard only flies when she is in residence. There is an annual summer opening of the State Rooms if you have children who would be interested in going round the Palace. This would let them get the feel of all the pomp and ceremony of a State visit and they would see many paintings from the royal collection, the Marble Hall and the White Drawing Room. You leave via the Bow Room and the garden where the Queen's Garden Parties are held each summer.

Buckingham Palace is open each year from early August to October 4th. There is a ticket office in Green Park which is open daily from 9am to 4pm and it is all so well organised. You are on a timed ticket and do not have a very long wait in queues–a most important point when taking children to such places.

The furniture and pictures are wonderful, perhaps not so much appreciated by the children, but the fact that it is the Queen's residence will be something for children and you to remember.

CENOTAPH

Whitehall, London SW1
age group: 8 - 15
how to get there: Underground - Embankment, Charing Cross, Westminster. Buses - 3, 11, 24, 77A, 88.

You might like to take older, interested, children on a tourist walk down Whitehall where they can see the Cenotaph where most school children know that wreaths of Flanders poppies are laid on 11 November to commemorate those who gave their lives in war.

CHANGING THE GUARD

Buckingham Palace, London SW1
age group: 5 - 15
how to get there: Underground - Green Park, Victoria, St James's Buses - 11, 16, 24, 52, 73, or on foot from Trafalgar Square so one walks up the Mall

This is a No 1 tourist attraction and it takes place daily from April 1st to the end of August at 11.30am and between September and March on alternate days again at 11.30am . Some children love the pomp and ceremony of this spectacle and many will be familiar with 'They're changing the guard at Buckingham Palace' by A.A. Milne.

DOWNING STREET

off Whitehall, London SW1
age group: 8 - 10
how to get there: see Cenotaph above.

As both numbers 10 and 11 Downing Street, the homes of the Prime Minister and Chancellor of the Exchequer, are constantly in the news, you can point out Downing Street while you are walking down Whitehall. It's almost opposite the Cenotaph.

FORTNUM & MASON

181 Piccadilly, London W1
tel: 0171 734 8040
age group: 5 - 15
opening times: Monday to Saturday 9.30am to 6pm.
how to get there: Underground - Piccadilly or Green Park. Buses - 9, 14, 19, 22, 38.

On another occasion you might want to enjoy the inside of Fortnum's with its red carpets and chandeliers. As grocers to the Queen this shop offers excellence in every way. For the children, if you're in the area, perhaps seeing the statue of Eros at Piccadilly Circus, there is the extra treat of Fortnum's famous clock which is a London landmark.

HAMPTON COURT

East Molesey, Surrey KT8 9AU
tel: 0181 781 9500
age group: all ages
admission: Adults £9.25 Children 5 - 15 £6.10 OAPs £7.00. The price includes admission to the Palace, gardens and maze.
opening hours: Mid April to mid October Monday 10.15am to 6pm Tuesday to Saturday 9.30am to 6.pm. Mid October to mid April Monday 10.15am to 4.30pm. Tuesday to Sunday 9.30am to 4.30pm. Closed Christmas Eve & Christmas Day
how to get there: Train from Waterloo direct to Hampton Court (takes 30 minutes).
Buses -111, 216, 411, 415, 440, 461, 501, 513, 726, R68. Sundays only 267 to the door
Boat - from Westminster Pier (3 hours), Car - M25 to junction 12 on to A308, Coach: Green Line from Victoria No's 415 & 718

Hampton Court Palace is the oldest Tudor Palace in England and was Henry VIII's favourite residence. The Maze here is the most famous in the world. This is a big day out. The admission price is quite high but there is much to see and do here.

There is no doubt that the best way to go is by train from Waterloo. The buses take much longer and by car it is approximately an hour but the journey can take much longer. There are plenty of parking spaces once there. You can also take the water bus which is great fun but does take a long time. See chapter seven

To 'experience' the Palace properly takes about four hours and that is before you visit the famous Maze which is a real must.

There are two restaurants, the Queen Elizabeth I Kitchen in the Palace and the Tilt Yard Tearoom in the grounds. Both serve quite acceptable buffet style hot and cold food. We opted for a picnic lunch and then had a cream tea in the tearoom which cuts down the cost and was a very good option.

During the school holidays Hampton Court runs special events for children which include mask making and model making workshops to name just two. It is definitely worth telephoning in advance for further details closer to the time of your visit.

HOUSES OF PARLIAMENT

Westminster, London SW1
tel: 0171 219 4272
age group: 8 - 15.
opening times: these vary considerably.
how to get there: Underground - Westminster. Buses - 3, 11, 24, 53, 77, 88, 159.

Only older children might like to take a look inside the Houses of Parliament. If they are keen, you'll have to plan ahead. Foreign visitors should apply to their own embassy. UK citizens will get the best treatment if they write, mentioning children, to their Member of Parliament. If you're in the area, perhaps on your Whitehall walk, or from the double-decker bus, you can point out the clock tower where Big Ben famously chimes. At the same time, you can show them the River Thames and Westminster Bridge.

KENSINGTON PALACE, W8.

tel: 0171 937 9561.
age group: 10 - 15
admission: Adults £7.50 Children & OAPs £5.90
opening times: Monday to Sunday 10am to 6pm last admission 5pm
how to get there: Underground - Queensway, Bayswater. Buses - 12, 88, 9, 52, 73.

The state apartments have been restored in the last few years and are semi furnished. There are guides that can explain the history of the palace and since the death of Princess Diana, Kensington Palace has become much visited so please try to visit early.

It takes approximately 1 1/4 hours to go round and at the end of the tour you will find an interesting, well stocked gift shop next door to the Orangery where they do lunches and teas in a beautiful setting overlooking the magnificent gardens,

B.F.G. *Queen Victoria was born in the palace in 1819. She reigned for 63 years and died, age 81, in 1901. It is possible to go inside the Palace, which contains some fabulously restored interiors, a new exhibition on Court Dress and a collection of the Queen's dresses, phone the number given for details.*

THE TOWER BRIDGE EXPERIENCE

Tower Bridge, London SE1 2UP
tel: 0171 378 1928
age group: 8/14

admission: Adults £5.95. OAPs& Children (5-15) & Students £3.95.

opening times: Monday to Sunday 10pm to 6.30pm. April to Oct, 9.30am to 6pm November to March, Closed Dececember 24th-26th inclusive

how to get there: Underground Tower Hill on District & Circle lines.

Buses - 15, 42, 47, 78, 100 or use the River Boat to Tower Pier!

The best part of the Tower Bridge Experience is the view. Once up on the walkway which runs from North to South the views are spectacular. The actual workings and engineering feats of one of London's most famous landmarks are remarkable.

There is a small gift and souvenir shop. The surrounding area is well served and you can have an interesting riverside walk down to the Globe Theatre and the new modern Tate Gallery. There are car parks in the vicinity but it might be better to arrive by tube and walk back.

LONDON BRIDGES

over the River Thames.
age group: 5 - 14
how to get there: by water, on foot, or by road!

How many bridges are there? There are lots! I reckon there are 22 bridges over the River Thames and it's fun to make lists of them, maybe have a notebook and write the bridges down when the children see them, or maybe hear of them.

B.F.G. *Going from East to West, the bridges are: 1. Tower Bridge. 2. London Bridge. 3. Southwark Bridge. 4. Blackfriars Bridge. 5. Waterloo Bridge. 6. Hungerford Bridge. 7. Westminster Bridge. 8. Lambeth Bridge. 9. Vauxhall Bridge. 10. Chelsea Bridge. 11. Battersea Bridge. 12. Wandsworth Bridge. 13. Putney Bridge. 14. Hammersmith Bridge. 15. Barnes Bridge. 16. Chiswick Bridge. 17. King Edward VIII Bridge, Kew. 18. Twickenham Lock Bridge. 19. Twickenham Bridge. 20. Richmond Bridge. 21. Kingston Bridge. 22. Hampton Court Bridge. Putney Bridge is the only one with a church at each end.*

SAINT PAUL'S CATHEDRAL

Ludgate Hill, London EC4
age group: 5 - 15
how to get there: Underground - St. Paul's. Buses - 6, 9, 11, 22, 25.

You might have already climbed to the top of St. Paul's. (See Chapter Five). If you have, and even if you haven't, most children would like a glimpse of this cathedral, designed by Sir Christopher Wren and built after the Great Fire of London. Outside, children could use up energy climbing up the steps. Inside, children with American connections would be interested in the chapel dedicated as a memorial to American forces in Britain. Lovers of the film, Mary Poppins might enjoy the visit - pigeons and all.

THAMES BARRIER & VISITORS CENTRE

1, Unity Way, Woolwich, London SE18
tel: 0181 854 1373 and 0181 305 4188
age group: 10 - 15

admission charges: Adult £3.40, Children and over 65's £2
opening times: 10am to 5pm weekdays 10.30am to 5.30pm weekends, closed Christmas Eve, Christmas Day and Boxing Day
how to get there: by rail to Charlton, or see below.

This is a day out for older children an outing that I got totally right for my grandsons who were aged 12 and 14 at the time.

We took the light railway from Bank Underground Station to Island Gardens, which takes about 30 minutes but it is fascinating seeing all the developments that are going on in the Docklands. Then we walked under the Thames (it's a foot tunnel) over to Greenwich and picked up a boat going up to the Thames Barrier. These run every half hour and the pilot gives you a commentary as you travel the 20 minutes it takes to reach the Barrier. The highlight for my boys on this trip was seeing the Millennium Dome half constructed and at such close quarters. The Barrier itself is a great engineering feat and an impressive sight–you get off the boat and spend an hour in the visitors centre where everything is well explained. After this enjoy a little sustenance and travel back on the next boat to Greenwich.

If it is your intention to make a complete day out on arriving back at Greenwich you can visit the Cutty Sark, then return on the light railway.

On this excursion there was so much to see and we took a picnic but there are many reasonably priced places to eat in Greenwich.

TOWER OF LONDON

Tower Hill, London EC3.
tel: 0171 709 0765
age group: 5 - 10
opening times: daily 9am to 5pm, Sunday 10am to 5pm (closes 4pm, November to February)
admission: Adults £9.50, OAPs £7.15, Children £6.25
how to get there: Underground - Tower Hill. Buses - 9 or 13 to Monument, then walk. 15, 25, 42, 78, 100, D1

You get a splendid view of the Tower from the riverside walk. Inside there's a massive collection of armour and uniforms and the Crown Jewels are in the Jewel House. The Tower gets crowded so avoid weekends and early afternoon and it is expensive, but worth the money if your children are likely to be interested in this slice of history where so many famous people have been imprisoned, killed and their heads impaled on stakes!

B.F.G. *The oldest part, The Keep, or White Tower, was built in 1078 by William Conqueror as a royal residence.*

UNITED STATES EMBASSY

Grosvenor Square, London W1
tel: 0171 499 9000
how to get there: by taxi, or by Underground - Bond Street and then walk.

If your children have American connections, they'll be interested to see their Embassy building which dominates one of the most attractive London squares.

B.F.G. *The Embassy was designed by Eero Saarinen the major architect and was completed in 1961. The American Ambassador's residence, Winfield House, Regent's Park, might also be worth a glimpse as it was donated by Barbara Hutton, the Woolworth heiress, to the U.S. Government in 1954.*

WESTMINSTER ABBEY

Broad Sanctuary, London SW1
tel: 0171 2225152
age group: 10 - 15
opening times: Monday to Friday 9am to 4.45pm, Saturday 9am to 2.45pm, Closed Sundays
how to get there: Underground - Westminster or St. James's Park. Buses - 3, 11, 24, 88, 159.

You can show the splendid outside of Westminster Abbey to children from the top of a bus, or you can include the Abbey while you are visiting the Houses of Parliament, which are opposite. Be sure they are really keen before taking them inside as hefty charges are now made. But, if they are singers, they might like to go to a service when they can hear the famous choir. Look in the press to find out times, or telephone.

B.F.G. *Elizabeth I, Mary Queen of Scots, Chaucer, Charles Dickens, among many others, are buried here and some of the monuments are very fine.*

WINDSOR CASTLE

Windsor, Berkshire
tel: 01753 868286
age group: 6 - 15
admission: Adults £9.50 OAPs £7.00 Children under 16 £5.00
opening times: Monday to Sunday 10am to 5.30pm (last tickets 4pm)
Random closure especially in November & December so it is wise to telephone the above number before setting out.
how to get there: Train-British Rail from Paddington to Slough, change

at Slough for Windsor
By car-on the M4 and follow signs to Slough and Windsor. There are two large multi storey car parks in Windsor.

A fairytale castle and all the more so for the children as it is one of the Queen's homes. There is much to see, the State Apartments, the famous St George's Chapel where they hold the Garter Ceremony and Queen Mary's Dolls House which is unique and which all children love. The tour lasts from two to three hours.

In the castle itself, there is nowhere to eat but Windsor itself has many eateries of all types. There are three gift shops inside the castle, two smallish ones and one larger, all selling similar souvenirs and gifts.

Try and combine this visit with the Open Top Guide Friday Bus which takes you on a round trip through Windsor and Eton and operates in the summer months. At the height of the season the buses run every 15 minutes otherwise it is every 30 minutes. The bus is a 'hop on and off' one, the round trip taking 55 minutes with an excellent commentary from the guide.

We had a lovely day visiting Windsor Castle and the bus trip enabled us to see Eton college and the famous Eton High Street.

The cost of the bus trip is £6.00 for Adults and £5.00 for OAPs, Children under 12 are charged £2.50. The phone number of the bus company which is based in Stratford on Avon is 01789 294466. They operate from March to early November.

If you feel you want help and a bit of a rest from coping alone with the children there are some very good guided tours that my grandchildren have very much enjoyed. Of course their individual tastes come into it. You certainly don't want to take a child who can't stand sport on a very sporty tour. Some of the days out that we have enjoyed are out of central London so I've also had to think about transport.

BUDGET TRAVEL. There are special offers for travelling round and about London. THE RAILWAYS offer joint tickets in which children travelling with an adult go very cheaply, sometimes for as little as £2 if you have a family travel card. Phone 0345 484950, at the cost of a local call, for details. Sometimes these tickets include travelling in London, on the buses and by tube. To find out about cheap travel and to get maps and brochures if you're not leaving London, go to LONDON TRANSPORT ENQUIRIES opposite platform 8 at Victoria Station. The office is open between 8.15am (Sunday 8.45am) to 7.30pm. They also have a 24 hour telephone answering service for queries about buses and tubes. The main TOURIST INFORMATION CENTRE of the London Transport Board is also at Victoria Station,

near platform 2. If you're a visitor to London, the chances are that your hotel will also be helpful with guides and advice. If you live in the capital you'll already know that travelling by car in London and its environs is a very mixed blessing. You can sometimes get completely gridlocked and parking is not easy to find and can be very expensive.

Eurostar to Paris

Waterloo Station, London SE1
tel: 0345 303030
age group: 10 - 15

I mention this as a big day out. It is fun to go to Paris on a train and experience the twenty minute under the channel part. It takes 3 hours both ways but you do come back knowing you have been abroad and experienced two of the world's great cities in one day. I cannot quote prices as there are so many different deals available depending on when you want to go but all information is readily available from both the booking office and most travel agents and at some times the costs are remarkably good value.

HINDU TEMPLE .

Brentfield Road, Neasdon, London NW10 8JB
tel: 0181 965 2651
age group: 10 - 15
how to get there: Underground - Jubilee line to Wembley Park then catch the PR 2 bus which goes direct to the Temple

I have included this as something unusual to do in our multi cultural society. When you reach the Temple it is as if you have arrived in India with all its marvellous colour and tradition. You must go to a service and children will love the spectacle and will remember it for a long time afterwards.

There are two services daily at 11.45am and 7pm. They only last 25 minutes so there's no time to get bored

LONDON WALKS

P O Box 1708, London NW6 4LW
tel: 0171 624 3978

The London Walks are many and varied. It is best to phone and get a brochure. There are just a few walks which are suitable for the older child - I would say over 12. I have taken my grandsons on one of the ghost walks, a little spooky but not too frightening. Then there is a Spies and Spy Catcher walk which could interest children of 12 to 15 if they have started to read spy stories or watch that type of thing on television. Then on a different note there is the Beatles walk and the Diana, Princess of Wales walk.

The guides for all the walks are fully qualified. Many are actors or authors who have written on the subject of the walk.

In the school holidays they do sometimes organise groups for children, but again do phone to find out what is on. I found them to be most helpful.

LORD'S CRICKET GROUND

St John's Wood Road, St John's Wood London NW8
tel: 0171 432 1033 or 0171289 1611
admission: Adults £7, OAPs & Children £3.50
Tours: 10am, 12noon & 2pm daily, No tours during Test Matches, Cup Finals and preparation days
how to get there: Underground - St John's Wood (10 minute walk) Marylebone Station (15 min walk). Buses - 13, 46, 82, 113, 139, 274

There is something wonderfully old fashioned about Lords. The day we went there was a county match on and there seemed to be a great many older establishment gentlemen with their MCC ties on wandering around the ground. It is impressive and from the moment you enter the W. G. Grace Gates you seem to enter a time warp.
The tour was instructive and we learned a great deal about the game itself.

It lasted between one and a half and two hours and to me the most impressive thing was the Long Room but you need to go on the early morning tour to see this as during play it is not accessible. We were fortunate to have this included in our tour.

There are catering facilities here but if you take a picnic, there is a small garden where you can eat or you can venture next door to the Lords Taverners pub where they had no objection to children and we had a good lunch.

The Museum is well laid out and informative. The famous Ashes are housed here and there is the Brian Johnston Film Theatre and the W. G. Grace Room. Although Lords exudes tradition, there are now some very impressive stands and a state of the art commentary position.

REGENTS PARK CANAL - JASON'S TRIP

60 Blomfield Road, London W9.
tel: 0171 286 3428
age group: 5 - 8
'phone for details of departure times.

how to get there: Trips begin at "Little Venice". Go by bus up the Edgware Road from Marble Arch, or walk - about 15 minutes.

There are three companies offering boat trips on the canal but Iam only going to mention Jason's Trip because it's my favourite. The boat is small and leaves Little Venice and meanders through London Zoo and up to Camden Lock.

This is not an overly exciting trip, but it's restful and you can take a picnic on the boat. The whole round trip takes about one and a half hours and it can be combined with a trip to London Zoo.

B.F.G. *The Regent's Canal is a very old and special waterway, a jewel in the heart of London.*

Speakers Corner

Hyde Park, London W1
how to get there: Underground - Marble Arch
Car - Easy to park around here on a Sunday morning.

Something of an institution on a Sunday morning when anyone is free to go to this corner of Hyde Park. An area has been cordoned off near Marble Arch and people can and do speak on any subject they wish.

For half an hour it is fun, for an hour it can be tedious. You get some real characters talking on politics, religion, sex, you name it. If you have a little free time on a Sunday morning, do go but only take the older children.

Twickenham Rugby Union

Whitton Road, Twickenham.
tel: 0181 892 8161 phone for times of tours
age group: 10 - 15
how to get there: by car along the A3 via Richmond

This is an out of central London trip but if you have rugby enthusiasts this is a must. It is known as the Twickenham experience. Your young are taken round the stands, the changing rooms, fitness centre and grounds. A Rugby Football Museum has recently opened which traces the history of the game since the oval ball was first picked up at Rugby School. (See also chapter Six, Activities and Sport.)

WATER BUS ON THE THAMES

tel: 0171 730 4812
age group: 7 - 15.
dates: April to September

A little like ordinary buses, you are able to get off these water buses at certain points along the river. They operate downstream as far as Greenwich and upstream to Richmond and Hampton Court. You can get on at Tower Pier, Charing Cross Pier or Westminster Pier. If you are feeling like a restful day and the weather is good, this is a lovely way to see many of London's landmarks. There is always a guide. Try to get on a boat where they only speak English, unless you're from Germany, Japan or France! Remember that children under 8 get very bored after a while on these boats, so keep this experience for them till they are older. Mine usually get restless after a couple of hours, but if you want to make

a day of it take a picnic to have on board and stop off at a place en route, such as the Cutty Sark at Greenwich, HMS Belfast, London Dungeons (See chapter FIVE) and the Tower of London. (See chapter SIX.) Consult the map and plan carefully when arranging this outing.

WEMBLEY STADIUM TOURS

Wembley, Middlesex HA9 0DW
tel: 0181 902 3333
admission: Adults £7.45, OAPs & Children £5.25
opening times: 10am to 4pm Summer, 10am to 3pm Winter
how to get there: Underground - Wembley Park on the Jubilee and Met Line, Buses - 182, 83, 92

I think this must be one of the best organised tours I have ever been on, they certainly have it down to a fine art but then the tours did start in the seventies.

There is an incredible atmosphere here and they have recordings of the crowds amplified on certain parts of the tour which helps to create the right atmosphere.

My two grandsons adored it, both being such football fans and supporters of Chelsea Football Club who have appeared several times at Wembley recently.

Every detail was explained to us, how the stadium is used for pop concerts and greyhound racing, how often the pitch is mown what the seating capacity is etc. There did not seem to be any part of the building which was left out. We saw where the television cameras and crew go, sat in the stadium, saw the changing rooms for the players, went up the famous players tunnel up to the pitch and finished up in the Royal Box with my young grandchildren holding the Cup–it all took about one and a half hours but not a moment of boredom.

Sadly Wembley is closing next June for a couple of years while they completely rebuild it–try and go before they close in mid 1999.

Useful Information

Some Useful Suggestions

(1) Disposable cameras are a wonderful way to get children interested in photography and to be more observant of what they are doing. If you are taking two or more children out have a competition to see who can take the best photos, it only takes a few hours to get these small throw-away cameras developed. This idea has been well and truly tested by all my grandchildren.

(2) All ages seem to love the itineraries (see page for examples) and it does save that old question 'What shall we do now!' I work on the basis that anticipation can be better than realisation. The quite young ones always seem to bring their itineraries with them and make sure we do everything to the written word.

(3) Keep all the tickets and the leaflets on where you have been and get the children to do a scrap book or collage. This idea has a dual purpose, it keeps them happy and amused and also helps them to remember what they have done and seen.

(4) You can have great fun in supermarkets especially if you are taking out more than one child. Give each one a list of what you need, a small trolley or basket, and a prize for the one who gets the list completed first. Try not to choose a peak time for shopping when doing this exercise as you will not be very popular with your fellow shoppers.

(5) I cannot emphasise this point too often - don't overdo the activities in the day. Lots of stops for drinks and a sit down. There is nothing worse than a seriously overtired child.

(6) Do try and do a 'dummy run' if you are having an organised time in London. Timing is so important with children, especially if they are working from one of the itineraries.

(7) Watch out for half terms and holidays - at these times everything will be much more crowded. Often the State schools go back before the private ones and this does ease the congestion at some venues.

(8) Cheap Theatre tickets can be obtained from a kiosk in Leicester Square on the day of the performance and a company in Covent Garden called London Theatre Tickets in James Street tel: 0171 240 0800.

(9) Take a small A-Z of London around with you.

(10) Always make sure you have an extra sweater or coat for them to change into, as there is nothing worse than children complaining that they are cold.

(11) When dealing with my younger children I do use a money belt as it gives you 2 free holding hands.

(12) Before leaving on an outing do telephone to find out if they have an unannounced closure or anything has changed.

(13) When going to the theatre, try to order your drinks for the interval before the show starts, there is nothing worse than queuing in the interval with children dying of thirst, not to mention the adult.

(14) Make sure children have some idea of what to do if they lose you, nothing more alarming for them or you if they are small. With older children try and agree a meeting place if you get parted.

(15) At all Museums and Galleries do go to the information desks to find out what projects are going on for children.

(16) Buy a travel card. Unlimited travel by Underground, British Rail, Docklands Light Railway and most buses. It is priced according to what 'zones' you want to travel in and how long you have. A special one-day off peak card covers all zones and you can spend all day travelling around London. Beware, you'll probably need a passport size photo of each person travelling.

(17) When on a boat going along the Thames ask someone which way you are travelling, as it is very easy to lose your bearings.

(18) Binoculars are another essential item you should consider when on a riverboat, as the drivers will often point out places of interest. There is also a lot of wildlife on the Thames, such as herons and cormorants - it would be a shame not to see them.

(19) Children enjoy feeding the pigeons, so include a spare crust or two in any picnic.

(20) Although it's a great idea to stick to any itinerary, try also to be spontaneous. It will give the children the giggles; as being silly often does.

(21) For the longer journeys (more than half an hour) take travel games such as cards or ludo and perhaps a number of crayons and some paper.

(22) London venues stage a number of sporting and cultural major events throughout the year so it is advisable to check your diary to avoid the busiest days in the year.

The Royal Tournament

PUBLIC TRANSPORT IN LONDON

Using public transport in London in many cases is not only the environmentally friendly option, it is also the quickest, cheapest and most convenient method of travelling around the metropolis. Free information is available from London Transport, two leaflets that are particularly valuable are The All London Bus Guide and Travelling in London.

TICKETS

On most occasions it will make sense to buy a pass or travelcard. If travelling on a bus, up to two children under 5 are carried free otherwise a children's flat fare of 40 pence is charged. Children aged 14 and 15 need a valid Child Rate Photocard, these may be obtained with production of a passport type photo and proof of age. Reduced fares are available for children on the underground, the price is dependent on the number of zones the journey will pass through.

PASSES AND TRAVELCARDS

To buy a pass or travelcard for a week or more a photocard is needed, come prepared with a passport type photograph.

Passes may be bought for use on the London Transport Buses network, price depends on the the number of zones included. These are available for a day, weekend, week or more.

Travelcards enable travel on buses, the Underground, Docklands Light Railway and trains. On Monday to Friday they may only be used after 9.30 a.m. Who would want to travel with children during the morning rush hour anyway? The price is dependent on the number of zones included. Available for a day, 2 day weekend (includes bank holidays), week or more. A family travelcard can be used for up to 2 adults and four children, this gives a further saving. It is important to note that all the people included on a family travelcard must travel together at all times. If you drop the children off anywhere it is not possible to use the travelcard without them. It is possible to buy a travelcard up to 7 days in advance, they can be bought from bus, underground and rail stations, or from a number of newsagents. Travelcards may be bought at railway stations throughout the south east. If catching a train into London, buy a train ticket and travelcard at the same time and save queuing twice.

One day LT cards are available which have no time restriction, and may be used on the Underground, Docklands Light Railway and on daytime London Transport buses.

Zones start with zone 1 which is the centre of London, and progress outwards to zone 6.

BUSES

The famous red London bus is known the world over. Two great plus points, there is often a bus that will drop you off outside your destination and the top deck is a great way to see London. As an alternative to a sightseeing tour use a pass and London bus guide. Many buses still have conductors who will let you know when your stop is coming up, and help with push chairs.

UNDERGROUND

A great way to travel, but avoid the rush hour. If using a push chair, a wide gate is provided. Those with push chairs may find access to the Underground available free from London Underground stations helpful, when route planning.

TRAINS

Some routes are useful for crossing London, in particular: - Thames Link service running through North London, the City, and south through Croydon to Brighton.

North London Line runs from Richmond in the south-west to Woolwich in the east, it is possible to transfer to a number of tube lines, rail services operated by Silverlink and Thameslink. If travelling to Kensington Olympia it may be easier to change trains at Clapham Junction (from the south) or Willesden Junction (from the north), so saving the bother of the tube. Using these routes may avoid travelling into the the centre of London.

REGULAR EVENTS

JANUARY:
London Parade
Chinese New Year

FEBRUARY:
Shrove Tuesday pancake races

MARCH:
Head of the River race

APRIL:
Kite Festival
London Marathon
Oxford and Cambridge Boat Race

MAY:
Canalway Cavalcade
Coin Street Festival
Covent Garden Festival
Highbury Festival of Music and The Arts
Museums Week
May Fayre and Puppet Festival

F.A. Cup Final

JUNE:
Croydon Jazz Festival
Dulwich Country Fayre
Spitalfields Festival
Stoke Newington Midsummer Festival
Tierra Latino
Trooping the Colour
Flower festival
City of London Festival
Henley Royal Regatta

JULY:
Hillingdon Borough Carnival
Hackney Show
Swan Upping
Greenwich Festival

AUGUST:
Ealing Jazz Festival
Notting Hill Carnival

Walpole Festival, Ealing

SEPTEMBER:
Covent Garden Festival of Street Theatre
Great River Race
National Trust Free Entry Day
Raising of the Thames Barrier
Thamesday

OCTOBER:
Punch and Judy Festival
State Opening of Parliment

NOVEMBER:
Fireworks night
Lord Mayor's Show
RAC London to Brighton Veteran Car Run
Remembrance Sunday
Christmas Parade

DECEMBER:
Christmas Lights, Oxford St. / Tree, Trafalgar Sq.
New Year's Eve, Trafalgar Sq.

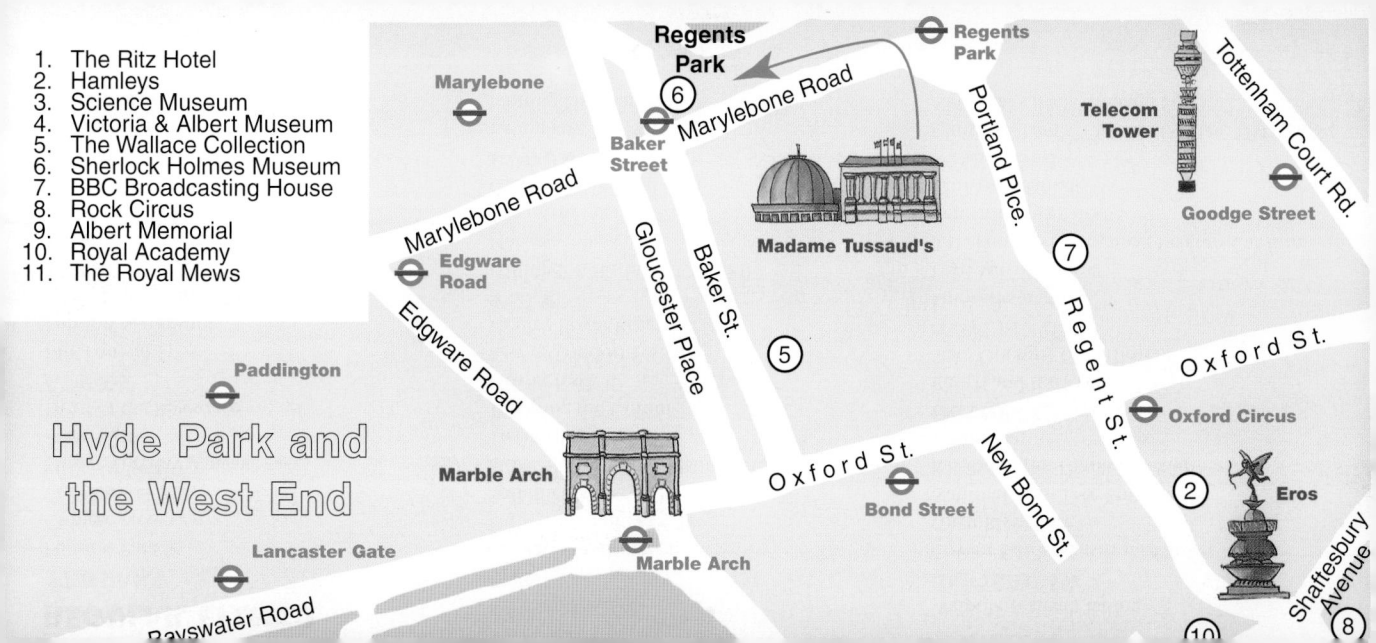

1. The Ritz Hotel
2. Hamleys
3. Science Museum
4. Victoria & Albert Museum
5. The Wallace Collection
6. Sherlock Holmes Museum
7. BBC Broadcasting House
8. Rock Circus
9. Albert Memorial
10. Royal Academy
11. The Royal Mews

Regents Park

Marylebone

Regents Park

Telecom Tower

Tottenham Court Rd.

Marylebone Road

Baker Street

Madame Tussaud's

Goodge Street

Portland Plce.

⑦

Marylebone Road

Edgware Road

Gloucester Place

Baker St.

⑤

Regent St.

Oxford St.

Oxford Circus

Paddington

Hyde Park and the West End

Edgware Road

Oxford St.

New Bond St.

②

Eros

Marble Arch

Bond Street

Lancaster Gate

Marble Arch

Shaftesbury Avenue

⑧

Bayswater Road

⑩

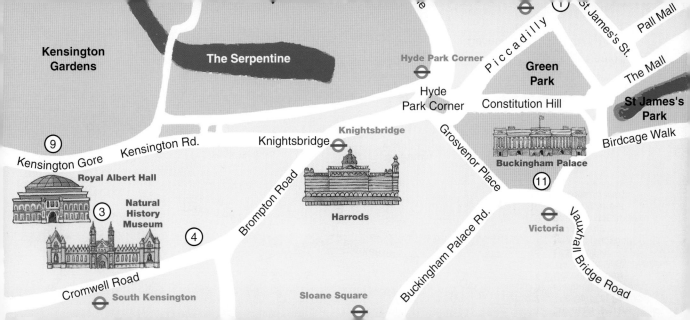

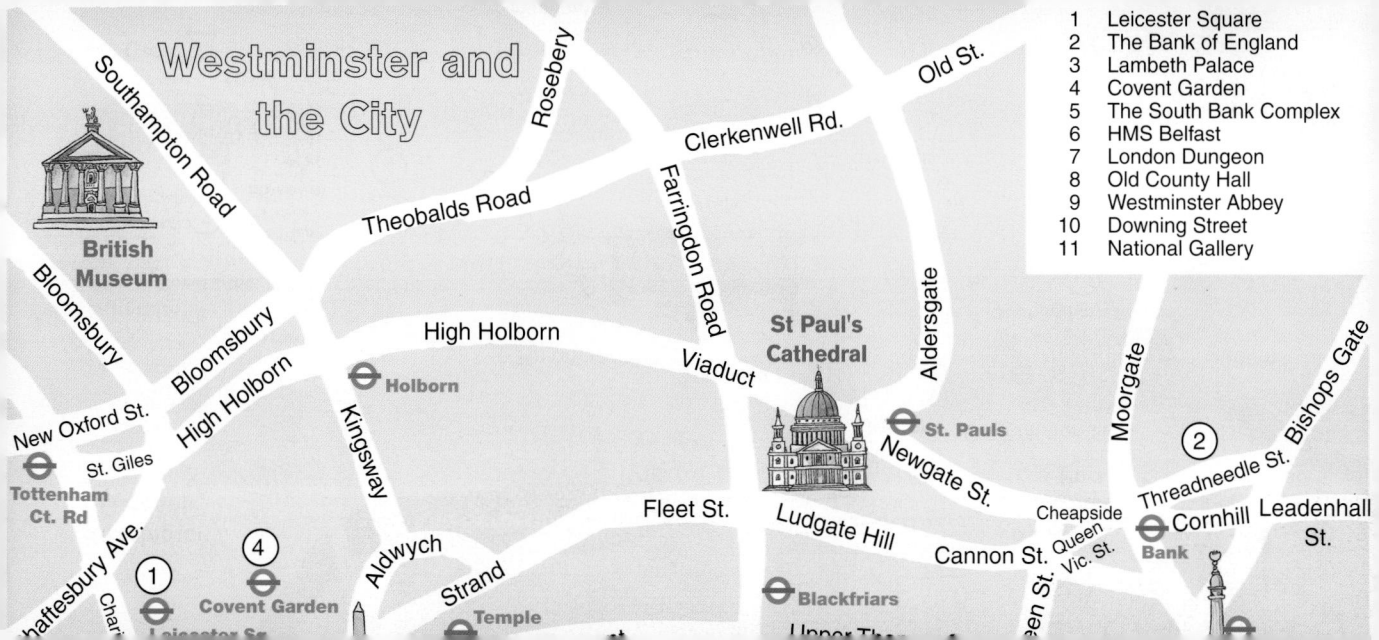

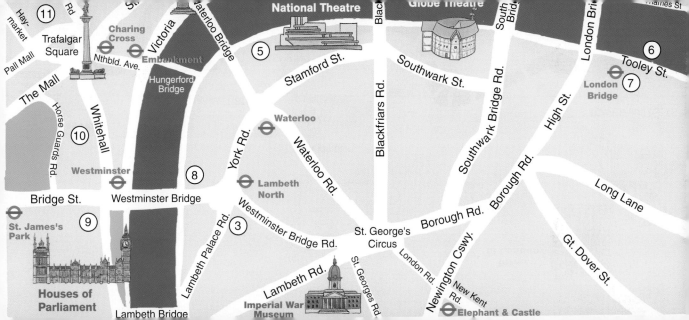

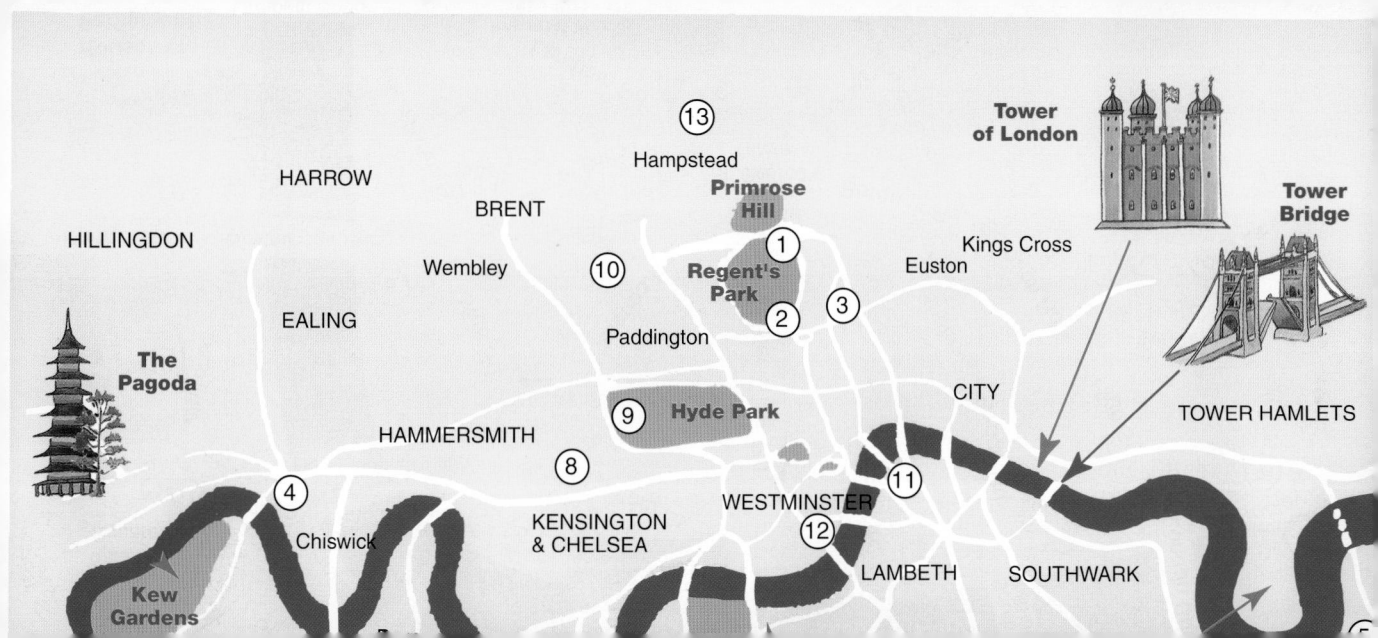

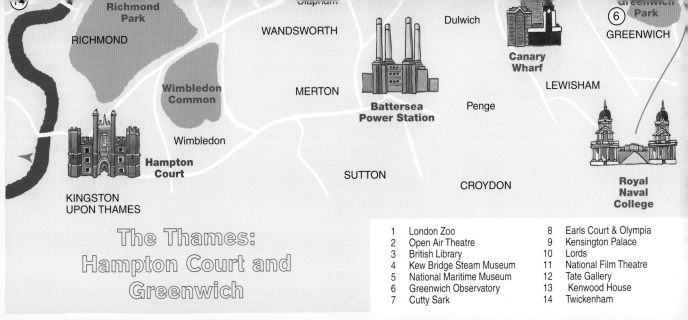

RICHMOND

Richmond Park

WANDSWORTH

Dulwich

GREENWICH

Greenwich Park

6

Wimbledon Common

MERTON

Canary Wharf

LEWISHAM

Battersea Power Station

Penge

Wimbledon

Hampton Court

SUTTON

CROYDON

KINGSTON UPON THAMES

Royal Naval College

The Thames: Hampton Court and Greenwich

1	London Zoo	8	Earls Court & Olympia
2	Open Air Theatre	9	Kensington Palace
3	British Library	10	Lords
4	Kew Bridge Steam Museum	11	National Film Theatre
5	National Maritime Museum	12	Tate Gallery
6	Greenwich Observatory	13	Kenwood House
7	Cutty Sark	14	Twickenham

INDEX